When Puppets Talk Everybody Listens

Shelly Roden

VICTOR BOOKS

a division of SP Publications, Inc., Wheaton, Illinois
Offices also in Fullerton, California • Whitby, Ontario, Canada • London, England

Second printing, 1979

Scripture is from the *King James Version* unless indicated otherwise. The other version
quoted with permission is *The New American Standard Bible* (NASB), © 1960, 1962,
1963, 1968, 1971, The Lockman Foundation, La Habra, Calif.

Dewey Decimal Classification: 791.538
Suggested subject headings: PUPPETS; PUPPET PLAYS

Library of Congress Card Catalog Number: 78-055265
ISBN: 0-88207-266-8

VICTOR BOOKS
A division of SP Publications, Inc.
P.O. Box 1825 • Wheaton, Ill. 60187

Contents

 **Foreword**

The Rewards of Using Puppets

Puppets can be an exciting and instructive addition to almost any home or classroom. Not long ago, I was traveling on one of our better known airlines. Often, the safety instructions given by the flight attendant are completely ignored by seasoned passengers.

On this flight, however, no one ignored the instructions because the flight attendant used a floppy green frog to remind us about our seat belts, oxygen masks, and emergency exits. In fact, we listened as intently as any class of preschoolers. When I looked around and saw everyone smiling, I was reminded again of the effectiveness of a simple hand puppet.

And then I recalled a kindergartner in a Christian school who would not say anything during the usual sharing time. The wise teacher made use of puppets. She allowed the child to put a puppet on her own hand and speak to the group from behind a cardboard stage.

Eventually, the child was able to speak to the class with the puppet on her hand, but without hiding behind the stage. And it wasn't long until she could speak in front of the group without any props.

While I was superintendent of a Sunday School junior department, I always made puppets available to the children. I used them to give instructions, correct a problem, or illustrate a lesson. One day a new boy arrived. He sat in a corner and wouldn't participate in any activities.

After talking with him for a few minutes, I discovered that he was very self-concious about his large front teeth. As it happened, I had a hand puppet with very large "buck teeth," so I told the boy that I had a friend in the classroom whose teeth were bigger than his.

He showed a bit of interest and, after the puppet had been placed on his hand, he went around the room talking with the other students through the puppet. As the Lord would have it, no one teased him about his teeth that Sunday and the battle was won. (Often afterward, I wondered if I had done the right thing because he talked so much from then on!)

I have been a "puppet nut" most of my life and have a collection of many different types—hand puppets, finger puppets, glove puppets, stick puppets, paper bag puppets—on and on ad infinitum. Furthermore, I have spent many hours in seminars, attempting to help parents and teachers feel free to use puppets in their homes and/or classrooms. The questions my students most often ask are, "Where can I get more information about the use of puppets?" and "Where can I obtain some puppet scripts?"

This book will be a rich source of ideas in both areas of concern since Shelly Roden has captured the excitement and challenge of using puppets. And she has included much practical information and many excellent, short scripts.

Mrs. Roden has the ability to put everyone at ease about using puppets. She explains that you don't need a special voice, stage, or expensive equipment. All you need to help you communicate through puppets is a relaxed excitement and sense of adventure.

Don't simply read this book—act it out! Buy or make a puppet and begin to practice as you read. I guarantee you a couple of things: At first, you'll be a bit nervous and feel a little foolish. But you will soon discover how simple it is to talk through puppets. And your reward will be having children—or adults—listen to you with new interest.

Puppets don't solve all the problems of communication, but they certainly do assist you in gaining interest and adding a little excitement and humor to the routine. I commend Shelly Roden for writing this book, thus providing a much needed resource for all current and future "puppet nuts."

James W. Braley
Director of Curriculum Services
Association of Christian Schools International

I
Puppets in the Classroom and Home

Using Puppets in Your Teaching

"I sure hope we get Mrs. Franklin for our teacher!" one child said.

"So do I," another replied. "She's neat!"

What teacher would not want to overhear a conversation like that between two of his potential students?

What is it about teachers such as Mrs. Franklin that makes them outstanding? For one thing, they are deeply concerned about their students. In the area of Christian education, they relate biblical truth to everyday situations so that children will apply it in their own lives. Furthermore, they vary their teaching methods and materials in order to communicate effectively.

Mrs. Franklin, for instance, skillfully uses puppets in her classroom. Her students appreciate and respect her because of her willingness to make learning pleasant and meaningful.

Puppets can be an exciting and delightful addition to your classroom too. They are not just another visual aid. They have the potential of "coming alive" in your hands. When you use puppets to illustrate a point, you are providing a semirealistic example. With a puppet skit, you can introduce a problem, illustrate its cause and effect, and present its solution. The following skit, "Consideration," shows how you can do this. Hoby is a hippo and Larney is a lion.

Figure 1
Hoby Hippo and Larney Lion in "Consideration"

CONSIDERATION

Characters: Larney Lion; Hoby Hippo
(*The skit opens with Hoby jumping up and down. His friend Larney finds his behavior very irritating.*)

LARNEY: Hoby, what are you doing?
HOBY: Jumping! What's it look like?
LARNEY: Well, do you have to do it in the house?
HOBY: Yep, it's fun!
LARNEY: Well, it bothers me. Besides, you're too big to jump around in here. Will you please stop?
HOBY: In a minute. Wheeeeeeeeee!
LARNEY: Cut it out, Hoby. You're making the whole house shake. You might get hurt.
HOBY: But it's fun, Larney. Why don't you try it?
LARNEY: Because I'm tired and—LOOK OUT!
(*A crash is heard and Hoby does not jump back up. After a few seconds he comes up slowly.*)

HOBY: Oh-h-h-h-h-h! I think I broke my foot.

LARNEY: Well, why didn't you listen to me? Oh, here let me help you. (Larney goes over to Hoby as if to help him.)

HOBY: Thanks, Larney. I'm sorry. I should have listened to you.

By using a skit like this you can set the stage for talking about the importance of being considerate, and what happens when you insist on your own way.

Sometimes children say things to each other that hurt. They need to be reminded that what they say and do can make their friends happy or sad. A puppet can help you get this point across, as illustrated in the next brief skit, "Fat and Dumb."

FAT AND DUMB

Characters: Teacher, one puppet
(Bring out a puppet, keeping his head down. Move his body up slowly as if he is sad about something.)

TEACHER: What's the matter with you? Why do you look so sad?

PUPPET: I thought Marty was my friend, but he just told me that he thinks I'm fat and dumb. Am I fat and dumb?

TEACHER: Of course not; we all like you very much.

PUPPET: Well, why do you suppose Marty said that? It really hurt my feelings.

TEACHER: I know. Sometimes others say things to us that make us feel very unhappy.

By using the puppet to illustrate the problem, you have shown your class that what they say to others really matters. Now you can turn to the children and ask them what kinds of things hurt their feelings. (Be sure to keep the discussion general so they do not end up accusing each other!) Through the discussion, help them see how God wants them to speak to each other.

The following skit, "The Best Tree Climber," shows how to teach the same truth, using the positive approach:

THE BEST TREE CLIMBER

Characters: Teacher and one puppet—Billy Bear

TEACHER: Wow, Billy Bear, you look so happy today!

BILLY: Oh, I feel so good!

TEACHER: Well, tell us about it.

BILLY: My friend Sam just said that he thinks I'm the best tree climber he ever saw. Isn't that neat?

TEACHER: It sure is, Billy.

BILLY: It made me feel really good! I didn't even know he knew I could climb trees.

TEACHER: That's great, Billy. It always makes us feel good when someone says something nice to us.

Figure 2
Author, Shelly Roden, speaking to Hoby in
"Fat and Dumb"

Telling children to be nice to each other might be more direct, but it would probably prove ineffective since children tend to be more concerned about their own feelings than about the feelings of others. The puppet dialogue helps them see another child's viewpoint. It grabs their attention and holds their interest. Furthermore, the dramatization of the situation has a more lasting impact because it shows as it tells.

If you've watched children watching puppets, you know puppets fascinate boys and girls (and grown-ups), probably because puppets are closely related to play.

Anyone who has observed or worked with children knows they love play. It absorbs great amounts of their time and energy. Children learn firsthand through play experiences. When you teach with a puppet, you're building upon these natural play instincts.

Children are also inquisitive. They want to learn new things—find out about the world and about themselves. When you present an idea with a puppet, you arouse their natural curiosity.

Even though they know you're making the puppet talk and act, they're fascinated. "What will teacher make the puppet say?" "Maybe the puppet will talk to me."

Boys and girls will be delighted to hear the puppet say something that you as the teacher or leader would not be free to say. Hoby Hippo can be funny, silly, or even rude in order to get a point across. Yet if you said the same thing, you might be out of character and could lose control of the class. Also, the puppet can be rebuked, corrected, or scolded as a nonthreatening example to the children.

Or, rather than your singling out a troublemaker in the group, you might have the puppet say something like, "I see someone who forgot his (or her) good manners." Through the puppet you are free to point out bad behavior without becoming overbearing. If the bad behavior recurs, a reference to the puppet's remarks may be enough to curb it.

Anytime you want to get the group's attention, a puppet can help you do it. Perhaps you're thinking, "But I have something important to teach; isn't that enough?" You certainly do have important truth to convey if you're teaching the Bible. And, yes, that should be enough. However, you must remember that TV, movies, and other amusements are constantly competing for your students' time and attention. In order to pass on your vital message to them, you must gain and hold their attention *and* communicate with them on the level where they live.

For example, children are often told not to be afraid of the dark. After all, there's nothing to be afraid of just because it's dark. But even as grown-ups tell them this, they are closing the curtains, bolting the doors, and turning on outside lights as if to chase the darkness away.

It's important for children to realize that they are not the only ones who are afraid. They should be given the freedom to express their fears, and then be encouraged to trust the Lord in fearful situations.

A puppet can be used effectively to help children admit and express their fears. If you wish to have them talk about these fears before moving into a Bible lesson, a puppet skit such as "Last Night in the Dark" can help your students honestly share their feelings. The skit immediately focuses the children's attention on the problem.

LAST NIGHT IN THE DARK

Characters: Teacher, Larney Lion
(Teacher brings Larney Lion out, moving his head back and forth as if Larney is afraid of something.)

TEACHER: Oh, hi, Larney. I'm glad you're here.
LARNEY: So am I. I thought I'd never make it.
TEACHER: Why is that?
LARNEY: I think I was followed.
TEACHER: By what, Larney?
LARNEY: Bad guys. I think they're gonna get me.
TEACHER: Why do you think that?
LARNEY: I think they were outside my window last night in the dark. I got scared.
TEACHER: I thought you were very brave, but now you tell me you're afraid.
LARNEY: Well, I'm *not* very brave. Aren't you ever scared?
TEACHER: Yes, sometimes I am. I think we're all afraid of something once in a while.
LARNEY: Really? Oh, it makes feel better to know others get scared too.
TEACHER: You know, Larney, I have a Friend who is always with me to help me when I'm afraid. Would you like to listen while I tell the boys and girls about Him?
LARNEY: Sure!

A puppet skit is also an ideal way to illustrate how sinful behavior such as lying, hating, stealing, or jealousy hurts God, others, and oneself. Of course, you must always be careful to be reverent in your presentation of attitudes toward God and the Bible.

"Where Is Freddie's Net?" with two mice called Teddy and Henry and a frog called Freddie, focuses on the problem of stealing. You could also use this skit as a springboard for talking about other sinful behavior.

7

Figure 3
A scene from "Where is Freddie's Net?"

WHERE IS FREDDIE'S NET?

Characters: Freddie Frog; two mice—Teddy and Henry
(Teddy comes sneaking on stage carrying a sack. He looks around as he moves, trying not to attract Henry's attention.)

HENRY: Teddy, I see you there. Why are you sneaking through here and what's in that sack?

TEDDY: (Drops the sack): What sack, Henry? I don't see a sack. (Looks around).

FREDDIE: (enters): Henry and Teddy, did you see a sack around here? It had my brand new bug net in it. I need that net.

HENRY: Teddy, do you know where Freddie's net is? Freddie, I think Teddy knows.

TEDDY: I don't know anything about it. Good-bye, see you later. (Teddy leaves.)

FREDDIE: Henry, I just have to have my net. I've gotta catch some bugs for my science project. If I don't, I'll be in trouble. O-h-h-h, what am I going to do? (Freddie leaves.)

HENRY: Teddy, come here this minute.

TEDDY: Here I am, Henry. What do you want?

HENRY: I'm sure you were carrying a sack in here a little while ago. Now, Teddy, if you have Freddie's net you better give it back to him. He's very upset. You don't want to hurt your friend, do you?

TEDDY: But I was going to use it for a little while. I didn't think he would miss it so soon.

HENRY: Aha! So you did take it! Freddie, come in here for a minute.

FREDDIE: What's the matter? Did you find my net?

HENRY: I think Teddy has something to tell you.

TEDDY: (Picks up sack and gives it to Freddie): Here's your net. I'm sorry I took it. I'm sorry I made you feel bad.

FREDDIE: (Sets sack down): I forgive you, Teddy. When I finish my science project, you can use my net.

TEDDY: Could I help you with your project?

FREDDIE: Well, I could use some help catching those bugs. Let's go. (They leave together.)

HENRY: I'm sure glad that turned out all right.

In this one skit alone, you have given an example of being sneaky, stealing, making the victim of wrongdoing feel bad, and telling a lie—on the negative side. On the positive side, you have an example of confession, asking forgiveness, being forgiven, cooperating, and sharing. You might follow a skit like this with a true-to-life application story or a Bible story.

Some children are quite hesitant about volunteering their ideas in a group situation. When a puppet is part of the lesson, these quiet children may be less hesitant about speaking up. One teacher of four- and five-year-olds has his children recite their memory verses to the hand puppet, Hoby Hippo. Hoby is able to get even the shyest child to speak up.

To be an effective teacher, you must be aware of the problems, concerns, and behavior common to today's children. Being observant and involved with children can help you develop this awareness. In turn, you will be able to meet your students' needs by conveying to them the message of God's love and His interest in them.

Using puppets in your classroom can be an effective way of attracting children's attention, holding their interest, and motivating them to listen and be more actively involved in finding God's answers to their problems.

Using Puppets with Your Own Children

As parents, you may find it fun to work along with your children in producing puppet skits, or teaching Bible stories with puppets, as described previously. However, spontaneous puppet play between a parent and young child has an even greater potential for bringing the child and parent closer.

It can give parents an opportunity to provide a positive example and give moral instruction—without lecturing. It also gives them a chance to find out what their children are thinking so they can communicate more effectively with them.

The following dialogue is an example of unrehearsed

puppet play between a mother and son. They are playing with the puppets Toby Turtle and Charlie Churchmouse. Blocks and other toys are in the room.

(The boy has the mouse and the mother has the turtle.)

BOY: I got a big mouse.

MOM: I see him. How did he get so big?

BOY: (Picks up a block that was in mouse's mouth): He eats giant seeds and things.

MOM: Oh, he must eat lots of them. Here come Toby Turtle. (Walks turtle over blocks.)

BOY: Hey turtle, get off my seeds. (Pushes turtle back with mouse. Turtle flips over on his back.)

MOM: Oh! Oh! I'm on my back. I can't get up. Help me!

BOY: No! You walked on my seeds and got them messed up.

MOM: I'm sorry. I didn't mean it. Oh, the sun's going to come out and I'll roast if you don't help me. I'm so frightened. Can't you help me?

BOY: The sun won't hurt you.

MOM: Yes, it will. I'll get too hot and then I'll get sick. Maybe an animal will come and attack me. Please help me.

BOY: Oh, all right. (Has mouse help turtle turn over.)

MOM: Thanks! That's better. I'm glad you decided to help me.

BOY: Just don't walk on my food again.

During this playtime the mother tried to help her child understand how a person or animal feels when in trouble. She suggested the importance of helping someone in trouble and gave her son a good example of saying, "I'm sorry."

Furthermore, she was able to use some words during the playtime that she wanted her child to learn. These words were *frightened* and *attack*. If the play had taken a slightly different turn, she might have used words such as *struggle*, *panic*, and *injure*.

A further advantage of spontaneous parent-child puppet play is that it allows the child's imagination to develop as he or she takes an active part in learning situations with his or her parents. Being able to think imaginatively can help children avoid boredom and assist them in applying spiritual truths as they imagine themselves in various situations.

Puppet play can even teach self-control. Children may give puppets whatever personalities they wish. They invent actions, situations, and language for their puppets. They are in control. This is important since children often feel powerless.

Furthermore, children can make puppets be bad or good in far more realistic ways than they can other types of toys. Such play may help children realize that, with God's help, they can control their own actions and attitudes. This realization is an asset at any age.

If you wish to provide creative, unstructured play for your children, you will find puppets are a good choice. A cuddly puppet friend can be made to seem alive by the child who owns it. The child can give it personality, playing out realistic or imaginary situations. In play, a child can learn and practice new words, values, and social skills, not to mention the fun of playing with Mother or Dad.

Here are a few situations in which you as a parent—or an interested friend or relative—might play with children and their puppets. You may want to add to the list as you think of things you'd like your children to be learning.

Suggested Situations for Parent-Child Puppet Play

A. Reggie Rabbit is being chased by Larney Lion
   1. Possible things that could happen:
      a. Reggie gets too tired to run.
      b. Reggie runs into a blank wall from which there is no escape.
      c. Larney trips and falls down.
      d. They run around the house and into each other.

Figure 4
A father and son play with puppets.

9

2. Possible values to teach:
   a. Understanding how others feel when afraid.
   b. Learning how to get along.
   c. Learning to help each other.
3. Words to use: frightened, worried, collide, chase, pursue, exhausted.

B. Suzy Squirrel has food but won't share with Reggie Rabbit who is hungry.
   1. Possible things that could happen:
      a. Suzy hides all her food so Reggie can't find it.
      b. Suzy goes and looks for more food and shares with Reggie.
      c. Reggie begs Suzy for some food.
      d. They both look for food and share it.
   2. Possible values to teach:
      a. Learning how to share.
      b. Helping each other.
   3. Words to use: Starve, hungry, cooperate, search, discover.

C. Peggy Panda feels bad. Everyone is making fun of her because she's different.
   1. Possible things that could happen:
      a. Suzy Squirrel and Reggie Rabbit invite her to their house.
      b. Peggy plans a party and invites the other animals so they will like her.
      c. Lester Lamb gets stuck between some rocks and Peggy helps him.
      d. The animals tease Peggy so much she cries and then they are sorry.
   2. Possible values to teach:
      a. Understanding how others feel when someone is mean to them.
      b. Helping each other.
      c. Being kind to someone who is different.

3. Words to use: tease, invite, help, friendly, unhappy, lonely.

D. Reggie Rabbit, Peggy Panda, and Suzy Squirrel all want to play tag, but Lester Lamb wants to play hide-and-seek.
   1. Possible things that could happen:
      a. Lester is left out and the others play tag.
      b. They play tag for a while and then play hide-and-seek.
      c. Lester gets mad and won't even play hide-and-seek.
      d. They decide to play some other game to which they all agree.
   2. Possible values to teach:
      a. Learning how to cooperate.
      b. Learning how to get along with each other.
   3. Words to use: pout, ignore, cooperate, agree.

E. Suzy Squirrel and Peggy Panda get lost in the woods and can't find their way out.
   1. Possible things that could happen:
      a. Suzy climbs a tree so she can see which way to go.
      b. Reggie Rabbit and Lester Lamb come to find them.
      c. Peggy looks for berries while Suzy looks for nuts and they share their food.
      d. Suzy and Peggy hear dogs barking and are afraid.
   2. Possible values to teach:
      a. Helping each other.
      b. Cooperating and sharing.
      c. Understanding how others feel when afraid.
   3. Words to use: lost, afraid, rescue, share, cooperate.

2
Choose the Right Puppets

Though children may respond favorably to almost any puppet you choose, they definitely appreciate seeing and using attractive puppets. Also, any puppet they will handle at all should be easy to manipulate, durable, and washable! Even though a puppet with these advantages may cost more initially, the benefits outweigh the added cost.

Each puppet should have a certain charm so that you can give it personality as you work with it. Having its own traits will add to the puppet's attractiveness. It will be like an old friend who shares feelings and ideas with the children.

Using a puppet with a growing personality in your teaching, will give your students something to look forward to. It can also help build group loyalty and be a big attraction in your Sunday School, Vacation Bible School, youth club, or class. You will find that the positive suggestions the puppet makes may be more powerfully motivating than yours.

Even if you've had only a passing interest in puppets, you're probably aware that there are many types available. You can buy puppets that are fairly inexpensive or you can invest large amounts of money in professional models, depending upon your purpose. It's also possible to make some kinds of puppets yourself.

When choosing a puppet, keep in mind such things as the size and age of your audience, how often you plan to use the puppet, and for what purpose you plan to use it. Almost any size or type of puppet can be used with a small group. But very small ones, such as finger puppets, would not be effective with a large group.

Finger Puppets

Finger puppets can be used very well with small groups of children. With young children, they can be used to tell a story, review a previous story, or help the children recall the order of a story's events.

Finger puppets can be made from various materials including paper, cloth, or plastic. Since finger puppets are small enough to fit in a person's hand, they are convenient to store and carry. Their small size also makes them suited for children to use at a learning center. They can help children retell a Bible story or other factual story or make up their own stories as a creative activity.

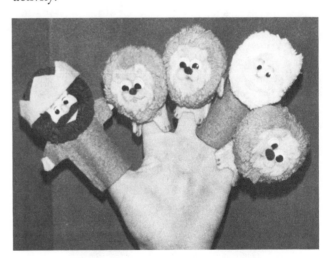

Figure 5
Pom-pom finger puppets designed to illustrate the story of Daniel in the Lions' Den

Figure 5 shows pom-pom finger puppets designed to illustrate the story of Daniel in the Lions' Den. The characters are Daniel, King Darius, and three lions. As the story is told, the puppets are placed upon the hand. They can be rearranged, removed, and replaced as the story progresses.

11

Since young children enjoy repetition, they may take turns placing the finger puppets on the teacher's hand as the story is retold. Or one of the children may tell the story while another places the puppets on someone's hand. This kind of activity gives children practice in recalling the facts of the story in their proper order and enables them to remember the spiritual application.

Finger puppets should not be used with large groups because they are too small to be seen easily beyond the first or second row.

Figure 6
Marionettes can be fun to make and use.

String Puppets

String puppets can be used in the classroom with older children if you want to provide an activity that is just fun. Children can use them to present a play or skit. But remember that the emphasis is on the operation of the characters as much as on the content of the presentation.

String puppets require quite a bit of skill to operate. Strings may get tangled and it is sometimes difficult to coordinate movements. But they can still be fun to make and operate and can be used as a creative handcraft. (See Chapter Four for instructions on how to make string puppets.)

Figure 7
A simple hand puppet

Hand Puppets

A simple hand puppet such as Peggy Panda is operated by placing one or two middle fingers in the puppet's head and moving its arms (or forelegs) with your thumb and little finger. In this way it is possible to move both the arms and head. Its arms can point, give directions, pick up objects, and simulate many natural gestures. When the puppet's speaking parts are coordinated with its head and hand movements, the audience gets the impression that the puppet is speaking.

Since a hand puppet's head and two arms (or paws) are operated by one hand, it must be fairly small (unless you have a large hand). This type of puppet can be used effectively with young children and small groups. If it is to be used with larger groups, it should be made of brightly colored material or have eyes, nose, and other features of a color that stands out from the basic color of the puppet.

Figure 8
Larney's mouth can be moved to synchronize with your words.

Hand Puppets with Movable Mouths

Another kind of hand puppet is one that has a movable mouth. The puppets Larney Lion and Hoby Hippo are that type. Your hand fits into the head of the puppet and makes the mouth open and close.

Since you are only concerned about movement of the mouth, a puppet of this type can be large enough to be used with almost any size group. Of course, the larger the group, the larger the puppet should be. Both animal and people puppets are made with movable mouths. When the animals are made of soft, furlike fabric, they appeal to young and old alike.

The movable mouth makes it possible for you to simulate speech by coordinating the movements of the puppet's mouth with the spoken word. Also, when constructed properly, the mouth is flexible enough for you to simulate many facial expressions.

It's possible to attach rods to the arms of hand puppets with movable mouths. The rods are operated with your free hand. This added arm movement makes the puppet's actions even more realistic and can help it exhibit a very believable personality.

The scripts and the other ideas for using puppets included in this book are well adapted for use with the two types of hand puppets just described.

Figure 9
A puppet with rods attached for added arm movement.

3
Bring Your
Puppets to "Life"

Before you begin to use a puppet in front of a group, you should learn how to handle it, preferably at home, by yourself. Practicing in front of a mirror is a good way to begin.

Since you want the puppet to become a personality, try moving it in ways and into positions that will be expressive. To show it is happy, move it around in a carefree manner and put its head up. To express sadness, keep the puppet's head down. Keep its face hidden if you want it to appear shy.

Make the puppet's head nod to show agreement or shake to show disagreement. Tilt its head when it is "listening." If the puppet has a movable mouth, it can be opened and closed to simulate speech. If the mouth is easy to manipulate, you may produce a variety of other expressions. Later, when you combine words, expressions, and actions, you'll see how lifelike the puppet can be.

Figure 10
The way you move a puppet can suggest moods and emotions, even personality.

When you are holding and working a puppet with a movable mouth, it will be necessary for you to drop your hand (see Figure 11). If you keep your hand up, the puppet will be looking at the ceiling instead of the audience.

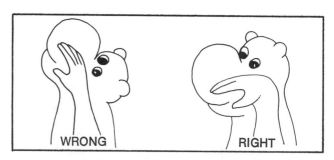

Figure 11
The illustration at the left shows the wrong way to hold your hand in a puppet with a mouth. On the right is the correct way.

Even when the puppet you are using is not speaking, it should move in ways that will indicate it is listening to you or to another puppet. You can have it nod or move just slightly so that it gives the appearance of being alive and interested in what is being said.

It's not uncommon to feel a little self-conscious when you first begin to use a puppet before a group. An easy way to begin is to make it look as if the puppet is whispering things into your ear. Then you relay these things to the group.

One music teacher uses a puppet to let the children know how they are singing. When the children are doing well, he says, "How was that, Sharpie?" He goes over to the puppet, picks it up, and has it appear to whisper in his ear. Then he tells the children what Sharpie said.

When the children are not doing well, the teacher stops and says, "What was that, Sharpie?" Again he puts the puppet to his ear, then conveys the message to the children. He might say, "Sharpie says you weren't singing loud enough" or "Someone sang the wrong words that time."

Children enjoy the suspense of waiting to hear what a puppet will say. By relaying what it says, you can be blunt, complimentary, or funny without endangering your position as the group leader.

Another way to get started using a puppet is to have it lead a song. For this you may use a simple hand puppet with a movable mouth and have it open and close its mouth to coordinate with the words. Or you might use one with rods attached to its arms and have it actually lead the singing by moving its arms.

A "listening" puppet can be of great help in getting children to speak up in a group or to the teacher. Some children are hesitant about speaking to the adult in charge. But a puppet can break down the barrier between the shy child and the teacher. One preprimary teacher uses a puppet to listen to the children's memory work. While the rest of the group is having songtime, children come to him one by one and recite their verses to "Hoby."

Figure 12
Hoby "listens" as children say their memory verses.

A second grade teacher uses a puppet to motivate the children in her class to review language rules. She simply walks around the room while the children are doing their desk work and has them whisper the language rule for the day to the puppet. She, of course, overhears.

When you feel comfortable with the puppet before a group, you will no doubt want to try to make it talk. You do not have to be a ventriloquist to do this. Children have good imaginations. All you need is a little imagination yourself in order to be effective.

One way to start is to have the puppet read a story to the children. A puppet with a movable mouth is especially good to use. Coordinate the words of the story with the puppet's mouth movements. Don't worry about the children seeing your mouth move; they don't expect you to be a ventriloquist. They will enjoy hearing the story by way of the puppet.

When you simulate speech with the puppet, be careful not to "bite off" the words. The puppet's mouth should open as the word is spoken and close as the word ends. Practice this in front of the mirror. Speak the words and make the puppet's mouth move as you speak.

The next step is to carry on a dialogue with the puppet. Before you do this, try changing your voice in different ways. Most people are capable of producing several voices. Find one that is comfortable for you and fits the puppet. Use it as the puppet's voice.

Don't be upset if you accidentally speak the puppet's part in your regular voice. If it happens, just go on. Mistakes are often more obvious to oneself than to others.

When you are carrying on a dialogue with the puppet before the group, look at the puppet. Don't be concerned about eye contact with the children. You already have their attention or soon will have. Figure 13 shows a teacher using puppets with a group of small children. You will notice that even though she is not looking at them, they are very interested in what is being said.

Figure 13
Boys and girls are eager to hear what the puppet has to say to the teacher.

One teacher of four-and-five-year olds tells of a Sunday morning lesson when the children would not listen to the story. She had a puppet with her and began to talk to it. The children continued chattering to each other for a short time, then noticed that the teacher was not even talking to them. She was talking to the puppet.

Soon all was quiet and the children were listening to the teacher and Squeaky the Mouse talk to each other. The teacher said. "Oh, Squeaky, isn't that rude of us to sit here talking just to each other and not to the boys and girls." The children were amused and ready to listen to the lesson.

You may also want to have the puppet carry on a conversation with one or more of the children. If you plan to do this, remind the children that they should use good manners when they speak to their puppet friend. Beware! If you have the puppet say funny things too often, you may excite the children and have trouble settling them down again.

Puppets can be used when conducting a Bible drill or a quiz time. These times are filled with excitement anyhow, and using the puppet to ask the question or give a reference can have a quieting effect. Just have the puppet speak in a very soft voice so that the children have to listen carefully.

Puppets can be a means of making newcomers feel welcome. Being new to a group can be a frightening experience for some children. Some are even shy about meeting the teacher. The puppet can be used to introduce newcomers to the rest of the group. When the children are in a circle or at their work areas, the puppet might say, "I see a new boy here today. Hi, Bobby, my name is Larney Lion. I'm glad you're here today," or "If you tell me your name, I'll tell you mine."

Figure 14
Larney Lion says, "If you tell me your name, I'll tell you mine."

You may use puppets to introduce a lesson theme. A very short puppet dialogue such as "Hoby's Family," which focuses attention on a particular subject, will suffice. For a lesson on the family, the teacher might use this skit.

HOBY'S FAMILY

TEACHER: We're going to talk about something everyone has.

HOBY: I know; I know—a big nose.

TEACHER: No, I'm sorry, Hoby, that's not it.

HOBY: A—a mouth?

TEACHER: No, no, Hoby. It's a family.

HOBY: Oh, can I tell you about my family?

TEACHER: Sure, go right ahead. (Enlarge the pictures shown in Figure 15 and show them as you and Hoby talk about his family.)

HOBY: (Show Hoby's Dad.) This is my father.

TEACHER: My, he's a big fellow, isn't he?

HOBY: He sure is, and strong too.

TEACHER: (Show Hoby's mother.) And who is this?

HOBY: That's my mom. She has her new hat on there.

TEACHER: (Show little brother.) And who is this?

HOBY: Oh, that one. That's my little brother, Happy.

TEACHER: Is he happy?

HOBY: Yep, always laughing, except when we don't get along.

TEACHER: You mean you fight with your brother?

HOBY: Well, sometimes we fight, but most of the time we get along with each other.

TEACHER: I'm glad to hear that. Hoby, would you like to listen while we talk about our families?

HOBY: You mean these kids have families too? Why sure.

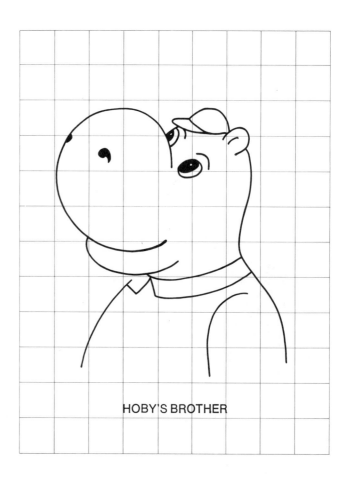

HOBY'S BROTHER

Figure 15
The grid over these drawings of Hoby's family is to aid you in enlarging the drawings. Simply draw your own grid with 1" squares (or the size you want your finished drawing to be). Copy the lines from the small squares in the book onto your larger squares.

HOBY'S MOTHER

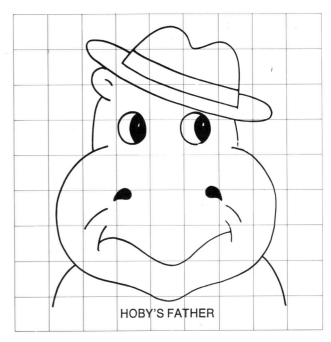

HOBY'S FATHER

When a session of Children's Church or VBS draws to a close, there is sometimes a time gap before the children go home. The handwork is finished, the papers passed out, the room straightened, and the children are waiting for Mom and Dad. Needless to say, things can get a little noisy. When parents come to get their children, teachers usually want them to get a good impression of their children's class.

Since children enjoy puppets, this is a good time for one of the teachers to sit with the group and review the lesson with a puppet's help or tell a familiar story with finger puppets or use the puppet to lead a song, say good-bye to the children, or invite them back again. As parents come, their child is excused and the rest of the group is occupied with a worthwhile activity until it's their turn to leave.

If you have a bus ministry, you can use puppets to encourage children to come to Sunday School on the bus. Someone riding the bus can teach a song or tell a story on the way to church. The same puppet may be used in neighborhood rallys conducted to interest children in coming to church on the bus.

When you have mastered carrying on a dialogue with a puppet by changing your voice to produce the puppet's voice, you might want to try ventriloquism. To practice forming words without moving your lips, tuck your tongue tip down behind your lower front teeth. This gives you more room inside your mouth for the sound to form. Keep your lips and teeth slightly parted and begin to speak.

You can say any word clearly that does not require you to use your lips to form it. Words that contain *b*, *p*, and *m* are troublesome. There are several things you can do about this. One is to avoid using words that contain these letters by substituting a synonym for the troublesome word. Instead of saying, "I'm a bad boy," have the puppet say, "I'm a naughty fellow." Or you

may rephrase the sentence completely. Change "I'm not very brave" to "I get scared."

Sometimes it's impossible to avoid a *b*, *p*, or *m* sound so you must direct the audience's attention away from yourself, toward the puppet. You may turn your head more toward the puppet and speak the word out of the corner of your mouth. Or simply drop the sound: "She's a very 'retty (pretty) girl." Substituting a sound similar to the difficult one is another solution: "I went out to "flay val" instead of "I went out to play ball."

Since the puppet is somewhat of a "character" anyhow, he will not be expected to say everything correctly. This will help you have the advantage as you attempt to be a ventriloquist. Incidentally, ventriloquists do not throw their voices. They simply direct your attention to an object and produce a sound that would be expected to come from it. This gives the *impression* that the sound is coming from the object.

Ventriloquism can be fun and everyone is fascinated by it. Children in third grade and up will enjoy your use of ventriloquism and also get the message during your dialogue with the puppet. However, when you use a puppet with younger children, it is best not to use ventriloquism. Preschoolers and young primaries are still sorting reality from fantasy and are quite capable of handling either separately. But by now many of them are fairly certain that animals and dolls do not talk in real life even though they do in some of their storybooks and playtime.

When you use ventriloquism, some of them will become confused. While you're trying to get the message across through your puppet/teacher dialogue, they'll be trying to figure out whether or not the puppet is really talking.

Afterward, some will even want to see if the puppet has a battery in it. One little boy of four asked the teacher if she would make "Chuckie Churchmouse" talk for him. The teacher put the mouse on her hand and had "Chuckie" talk to him. "No," he said, "I want Chuckie to talk to me; on my hand." This could have been avoided if the teacher had let the children know that she was making the puppet talk.

Another way of simulating puppet speech for a puppet/teacher dialogue is by using a tape recorder. You can choose anyone you wish to be the puppet's voice. With a script in front of you and the person you have chosen, start the tape recorder. Read your part silently. When you want your partner to speak his part, point to him. He will then read his part aloud into the recorder. Again, you will read your part silently and repeat this process until you have taped the entire script.

Be sure to play the tape back right away to see if you have given yourself enough time to say your part aloud. You may need to retape your script until it is right. When you are ready to present your dialogue, your helper, who will be hidden from view behind a puppet stage, will play the tape and move the puppet in accordance with the taped speaking part. You may wish to either memorize your part or hold a small card with your cues written on it and glance at it when necessary. Or, by placing a small puppet fence on a tabletop, you may present the whole thing yourself, using the fence to hide your tape recorder.

Figure 16
An improvised stage, using a "puppet fence" to hide a tape recorder.

If you intend to present a fairly long skit or puppet play, you may want to tape record it. Recording the spoken parts allows the puppeters to concentrate on moving the puppets realistically. And since just moving the puppets takes a fair amount of time and practice, that's an important consideration. Furthermore, it is very strenuous to hold a puppet overhead while kneeling inside the stage.

For short presentations you may tack the written script inside the puppet stage so the puppeteers can read their parts as they move the puppets. Standing to one side, you can interact with the puppets by having your helpers either read their parts from a prepared script or, if your helpers are experienced and confident, you may interact spontaneously with the puppets.

If you are going to use a puppet stage for your presentation, you should be aware of some possible problems. As soon as children see a puppet stage, they get excited. They know something unusual is about to happen and hope to be entertained.

If your performance is too slapstick, they may become so excited that the meaning and lesson in the skit will be lost on them. Unless you are using the puppet performance strictly for entertainment, it is better to minimize comedy routines. You can still use humor, but temper it to your purpose.

Another caution that applies to using puppets in the church is of great importance and sometimes overlooked by the most well-meaning teacher. Be extremely careful not to have an animal puppet talk about his being personally related to God.

It may appeal to children to have the puppet experience salvation, pray, or quote Scripture, but it will be something they will have to unlearn later. Animals and other pretend characters do not relate to God. Even a person puppet should not express a personal relationship to God in a puppet/teacher dialogue, since this may confuse some children.

Any puppet can, however, express an interest in listening to a story, make a comment on the facts of the lesson, ask a question about a Bible story or character, give a Bible reference during a Bible drill, or illustrate positive or negative attitudes and actions. Also, a full-blown puppet play which depicts a Bible story or life application story and uses people puppets may be used to tell a story very effectively. The puppet would then be "in character" and acting in accordance with the facts of the story.

So you see you can choose from a variety of methods in working with puppets. Just be sure that the one you choose is best for your particular teaching situation whether in Sunday School, club work, school, or at home. And do start out simply, after practice in private, so that you have a measure of confidence when you appear in public.

4
You Can Make
Your Own Puppets

Making puppets can be a lot of fun for both adults and children. Puppet clubs and other organizations often make their own, and then present plays. And for children, puppet-making can be a worthwhile, creative craft or art project. It not only allows them to make something, but allows them to create a personality for it.

However, puppet-making is time-consuming and can be costly, especially if you intend to make puppets that are appealing and durable. Furthermore, patterns for puppets are not always easy to find. So before attempting to make your own, do see what you can buy.

You might check toy or hobby stores, Christian bookstores, or Sunday School supply houses. If, after investigating these sources, you decide to make your own, consider using the patterns provided in the following pages.

POM-POM FINGER PUPPETS

SHAGGY DOG

GIRAFFE STRING PUPPET

Figure 17
All of these are puppets you can make by following the directions on the next pages.

PARROT STRING PUPPET

Puppets You Can Make

Pom-pom Finger Puppets for Daniel in the Lions' Den

Materials needed:

(Most of these can be purchased either at a fabric store or craft shop.)

Two-inch pom-poms: 1 white, 2 brown, 3 orange

Felt scraps: Pink for faces and hands, yellow for lion bodies and faces, king's crown. Choice of colors for Daniel's and king's clothing. Brown and white for mustaches.

Thick white fabric glue (regular white glue is too thin and has a tendency to soak through fabric and stain it).

Wiggle eyes: Six ⅜″ eyes for lions
Four ½″ eyes for people

Directions:

Daniel and the King

Cut out felt parts according to the patterns provided. Glue faces to center of white or brown pom-pom. Stitch the finger form on the dotted line. Glue the pom-pom head, the clothes, and the hands to the finger form. Glue on eyes and mustaches.

Lions

Cut out lion parts. Glue the face parts to the orange pom-pom. Glue on eyes. Stitch lion finger form on dotted line. Glue pom-pom to finger form. Additional patterns are included on the pattern sheet for boy and girl finger puppets, Figure 27.

Shaggy Dog or Monster Puppet

1. Fur fabric for this puppet may be purchased at a fabric store. Felt and eyes may be obtained at a craft shop. You will need ⅓ yard of fur fabric. This will be more than enough for one puppet. Enlarge the pattern, following instructions in Figure 15. (One small square equals one inch.)
2. Trace the head, paws, body, and ears onto the back of the fur fabric from the enlarged pattern. Use a felt-tip marker or chalk for tracing. Be sure to reverse the head when you trace the second side so you will not have two of the same side.
3. With a sharp pair of scissors, cut out the parts. Cut only through the fabric backing so that you do not clip the long hairs if you are using a long shag fabric. Cut ear linings, mouth, and tongue from felt.
4. Sew felt lining to right sides of ears. Leave an opening between the notches for turning. Turn ears right sides out. Handstitch to close opening. Top-stitch ears to outside of head on stitching line. For monster, eliminate ears completely. Match darts on head and stitch. Place right sides of head together, matching notches, and stitch on wrong side. Leave the bottom open.
5. Sew body, right sides together, leaving armholes open. Also leave top of body or neck open. With right sides together, stitch head to body, matching front and back seams of head to front and back notches on the body.
6. Match the large dot on the felt mouth to the upper seam opening on head. Match the small dot on mouth to the center chin seam. Medium dots should line up with the corners of the mouth opening. Stitch mouth in place. Cut out the mouth backing from a piece of cardboard using smaller mouth pattern. Score cardboard mouth on dotted line. Spread thick white fabric glue on cardboard backing and glue it in place on wrong side of mouth, matching dots and score line with mouth corners. Let dry.
7. Fold paws right sides together and stitch. Leave open at top of arm. Stuff paws lightly with polyester stuffing. While puppet body is still wrong side out, insert upper end of paw into armhole opening of body. Make sure the thumb of the paw is up. Stitch through all thicknesses. Turn puppet right side out. Glue tongue into mouth. Glue on large wiggle eyes or attach half-round frog type eyes. Glue on one-inch pom-pom for nose.

Parrot String Puppet

Materials needed:

- One 4″ styrofoam ball
- One 2½″ styrofoam ball
- One styrofoam egg, 6¼″ long
- Two 2″ green pom-poms
- Two 1″ yellow pom-poms
- Two 9″ x 12″ pieces of yellow felt
- Two 1½″ metal rings
- Two 30mm wiggle eyes
- One felt sailor hat
- One 13″ x 8″ piece of green shag fur—body
- One 12″ x 6″ piece of green shag fur—head
- One 2½″ x 12″ piece of green shag fur—neck
- One package large green feathers
- Nylon filament and long needle
- Heavy white fabric glue
- Two wooden sticks 18″ and 12″
- Long straight pins and corsage pins
- Stiff floral wire
- Floral tape

Directions:

1. Cut off the ends of the 2½″ ball. Cut two 2½″ fur circles from 2½″ x 12″ piece of fur. Make sure you have 8″ of fur left to wrap side of neck piece. String egg and balls and fur circles as shown. Use a long floral wire to draw nylon filament through egg. Knot ends of filament and glue to secure. Glue fur circles to ends of 2½″ x 8″ piece of fur. Glue 13″ x 18″ fur to egg. Make pleats at ends to take up fullness. Secure with glue and pins. Do the same for the 4″ ball to form the head.

PEOPLE FINGER FORM

FOLD LINE

LION FINGER FORM

FOLD LINE

SIDE NOSE

NOSE

EYE SIZE

EAR

LION'S FACE

MUSTACHE

MAN'S COAT
(cut two)

MAN'S HAND

(allow hand below solid line to stick out of sleeve)

MAN'S FACE

EYE SIZE

KING DARIUS' CROWN

Figure 18
Pom-pom finger puppet patterns (actual size)

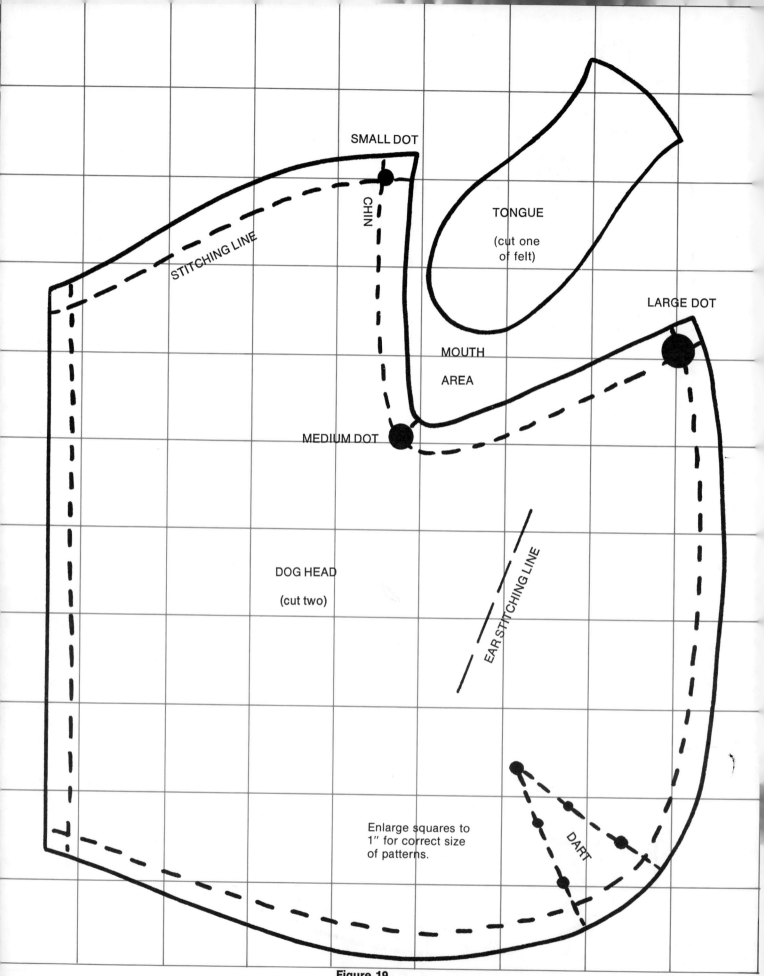

SMALL DOT

CHIN

STITCHING LINE

TONGUE

(cut one of felt)

LARGE DOT

MOUTH

AREA

MEDIUM DOT

DOG HEAD

(cut two)

EAR STITCHING LINE

Enlarge squares to 1″ for correct size of patterns.

DART

Figure 19
Shaggy dog pattern can also be used for monsters.

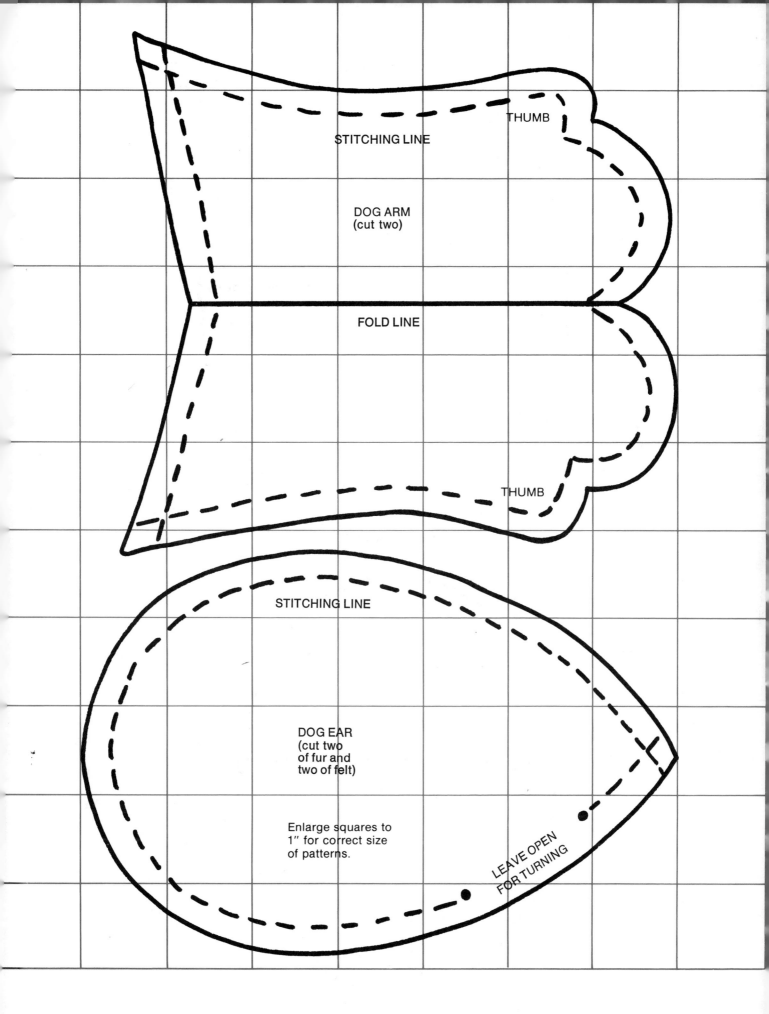

THUMB

STITCHING LINE

DOG ARM
(cut two)

FOLD LINE

THUMB

STITCHING LINE

DOG EAR
(cut two
of fur and
two of felt)

Enlarge squares to
1″ for correct size
of patterns.

LEAVE OPEN
FOR TURNING

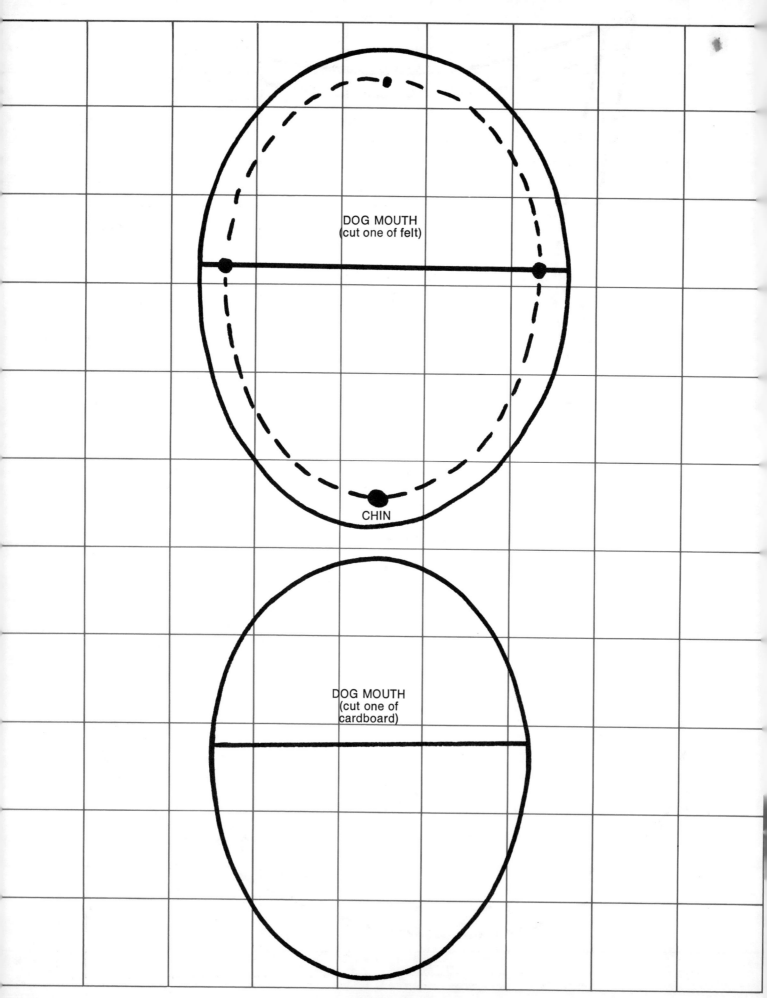

DOG MOUTH
(cut one of felt)

CHIN

DOG MOUTH
(cut one of
cardboard)

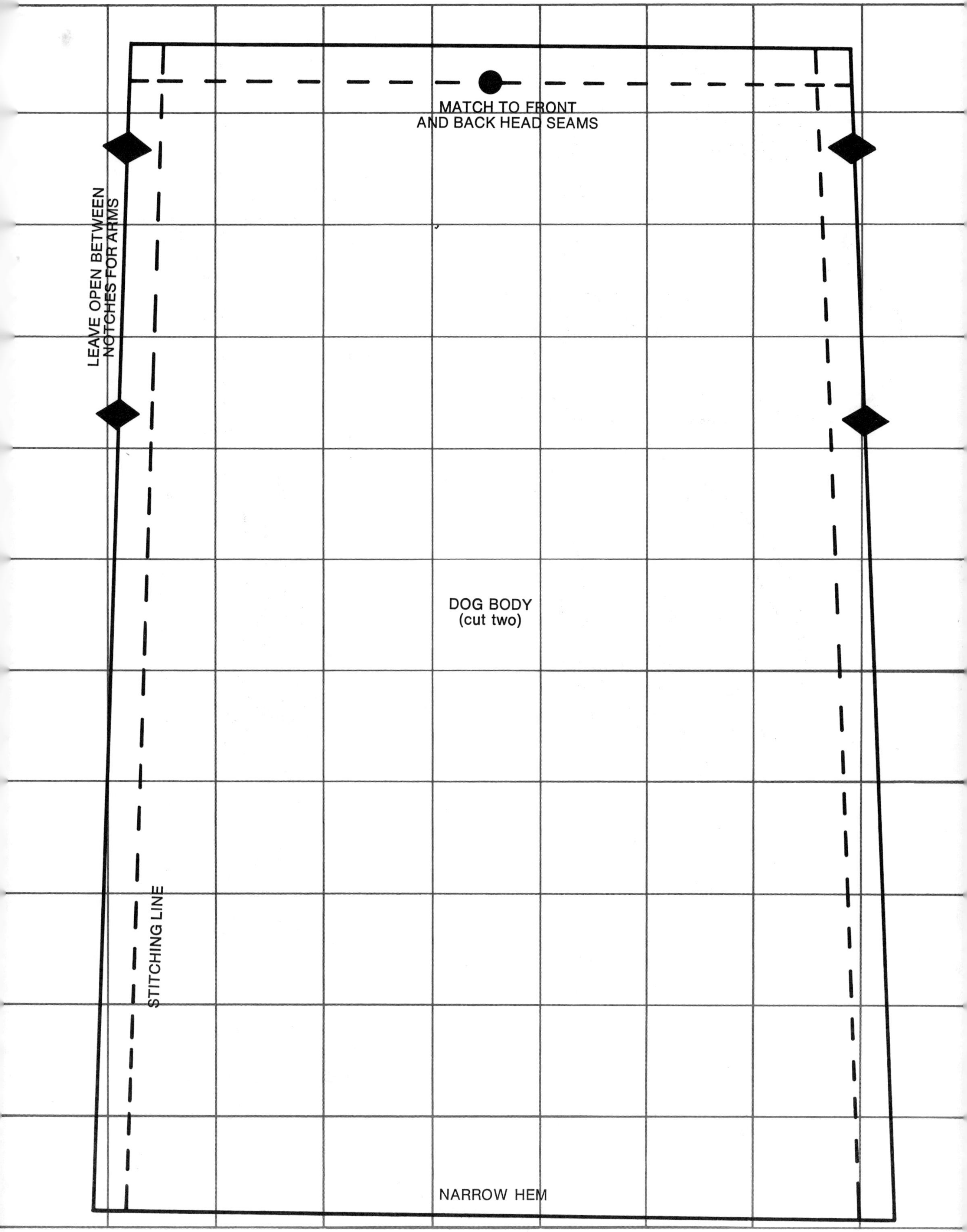

MATCH TO FRONT
AND BACK HEAD SEAMS

LEAVE OPEN BETWEEN
NOTCHES FOR ARMS

STITCHING LINE

DOG BODY
(cut two)

NARROW HEM

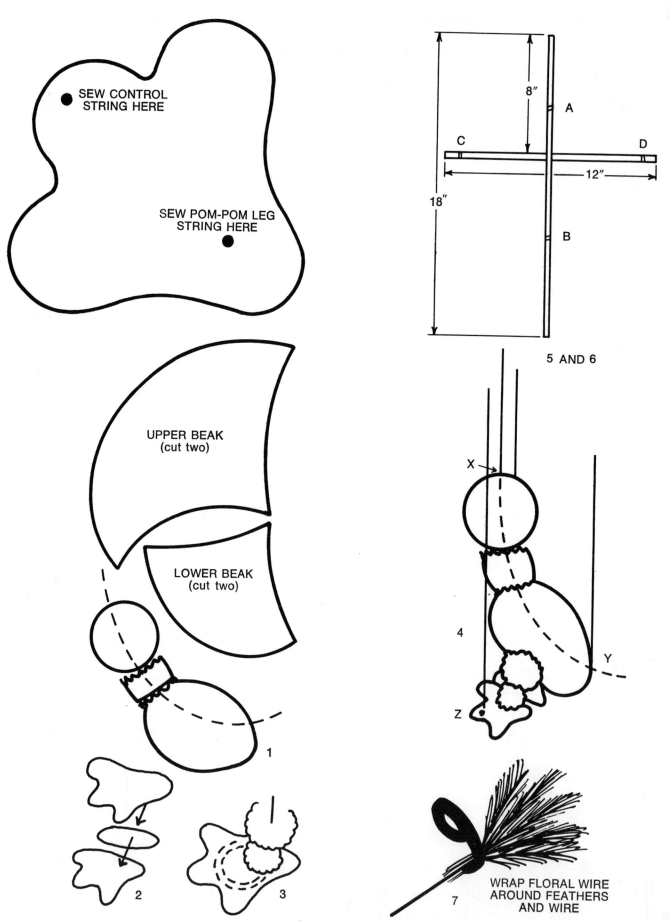

SEW CONTROL
STRING HERE

SEW POM-POM LEG
STRING HERE

8"

A

C   D

12"

18"

B

5 AND 6

UPPER BEAK
(cut two)

LOWER BEAK
(cut two)

X

4

Y

Z

1

2

3

7

WRAP FLORAL WIRE
AROUND FEATHERS
AND WIRE

**Figure 20
Parrot string puppet**

2. Cut two pieces of felt for each foot according to pattern provided. Glue pieces together with two 1½" metal rings in between.
3. Thread needle with nylon filament and sew from bottom of foot up through the ring and through the yellow and green pom-poms.
4. Glue and pin legs into body sides toward the back.
5. Glue wooden sticks as shown. Attach small screw eyes to sticks at points A, B, C, D. To attach string to body, push a corsage pin part of the way into the styrofoam where you wish to attach string (preferably at top of head X, at tail Y, and on feet Z). Tie string to pin and put some glue on it. Push pin into place.
6. Cut each nylon string longer than finished lengths and adjust length as you attach strings to sticks.
7. Cut parrot beak from yellow felt. Glue the edges and let dry. Insert a ¾" pom-pom into top beak to give it shape. Insert a ½" pom-pom into bottom beak. Pin parrot beak into place and glue to secure. Glue on wiggle eyes. Use five or six feathers for tail. Gather feathers around a piece of wire and wrap with floral wire. Spot with glue to secure. Attach tail by pushing wire into egg. Glue on feathers for wings. A small red feather may be added to the top of each wing. Glue hat on head.

Pom-pom Giraffe String Puppet

Materials needed:
- Three 2" yellow pom-poms—2 for body; 1 for head
- Three 1½" yellow pom-poms—1 for body; 1 for nose; 1 for base of neck
- Four 1½" orange pom-poms—for feet
- Seven 1" yellow pom-poms—4 for knees; 3 for neck
- Twenty-nine ½" yellow pom-poms—3 for neck; 7 for each front leg; 6 for each back leg
- Two ¼" orange pom-poms—for horn tips
- One 9" x 12" orange felt—for spots and ear linings
- One 2" x 3" scrap yellow felt—for ears and horns
- Four 1" diameter metal rings or washers—for bottoms of feet
- One ½" x 9" strip of orange fake fur—for mane and tail
- Nylon filament and long needle
- Six screw eyes
- Heavy white glue
- Two ⅜" wiggle eyes

Directions:

1. String body parts and head together, using nylon filament. Spot each pom-pom with glue to secure. Trim body and head to shape.
2. String legs starting with 1½" orange pom-pom; then three ½" yellow; one 1" yellow pom-pom for knee; three ½" pom-poms for back legs and four ½" yellow pom-poms for front legs. Glue metal rings or washers on bottoms of feet.

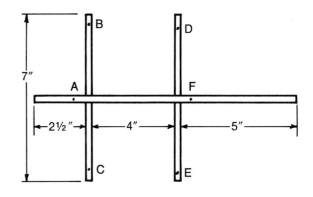

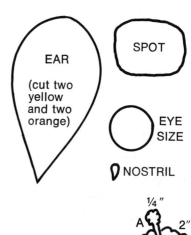

EAR
(cut two yellow and two orange)

SPOT

EYE SIZE

NOSTRIL

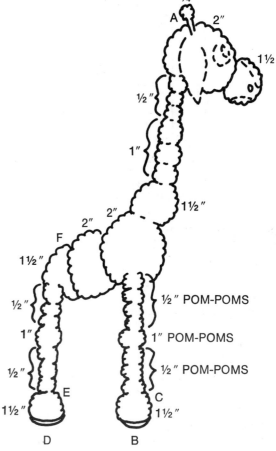

½" POM-POMS

1" POM-POMS

½" POM-POMS

Figure 21
Pom-pom giraffe string puppet

3. Glue control sticks together as shown. Attach screw eyes at points A, B, C, D, E, F.
4. Attach control strings: Cut each string 3″ longer than finished lengths which are given.
   - 16″ for head; attached to point A.
   - 28½″ for each leg; attached to points B, C, D, and E.
   - 23½″ long for body back; attached to point F
5. Cut ½″ orange spots from felt and glue to body. Roll small piece of yellow felt and secure with glue for horns. Glue ¼″ pom-pom to horn tip. Cut ears according to pattern, two yellow and two orange. Glue orange and yellow ear sections together. Attach to head. Trim strip of fake fur to 7″ length and glue on neck for mane. Trim remaining piece of fur and attach for tail. Glue on wiggle eyes and small orange nostrils.

Puppets Children Can Make

Figure 22
Paper bag puppet

Paper Bag Puppets
Materials needed:
- Paper bag
- Craft glue
- Crayons
- Scraps of fake fur, if desired

Directions:
A paper bag puppet can be made using prepared patterns which the children may color, cut out, and glue to the bag, or they can draw their own characters and decorate the bag as they wish. In order for the puppet to simulate speech, cut the picture of the face at the mouth line and glue the top part of the face to the bottom of the bag. Glue the bottom part of the face under the top part on the main part of the bag. (See Figure 22.)

Figure 23
Paper plate stick puppets

Paper Plate Stick Puppet
Materials needed:
- Heavy duty paper plate
- Flat stick at least 11″ long
- Construction paper, material scraps, etc.
- Craft glue

Directions:
Draw a face on the paper plate. Add construction-paper hair, eyes, nose, and mouth. Glue stick to back of plate. Add body if desired. (See Figure 23.)

.**Figure 24**
Paper cup puppet

Paper Cup Puppet
Materials needed:
- Large paper cup
- Craft glue
- Construction paper

Directions:
Cover cup with construction paper. Add hair and facial features. Draw and cut out a body and glue or staple it to the cup. (See Figure 24.)

Box Puppet

Materials needed:
- Two gelatin or pudding boxes. (Be sure to open boxes carefully so as not to rip off the long flap. You will need it to make a hinge for the puppet's mouth.)
- Craft glue
- Construction paper or fabric scraps

Directions:

Remove flaps on boxes except for one long flap on one box. With the two boxes held together, fold long flap into matching opening of other box. Glue it down. Boxes will now be attached to each other, hinged in the middle. By placing four fingers in one box and your thumb in the other, you can make your puppet move its mouth. Finish the puppet by covering it with construction paper or material scraps. Attach a piece of

Figure 25
Box puppet

paper or fabric to the back of your puppet's neck to cover your hand. Add teeth, eyes, etc. (See Figure 25.)

Felt Hand Puppets

Materials needed:
- Two 9" x 12" pieces of felt and a few felt scraps
- Heavy white fabric glue
- Needle and thread

Directions:

Enlarge pattern provided and cut out the front and back of puppet. Cut out face from pink felt. Cut hair from color of your choice. Glue or sew basic puppet shape together on dotted line. When puppet is dry or sewed, glue on face. Add eyes, hair, nose, mouth, etc. (See Figure 26.)

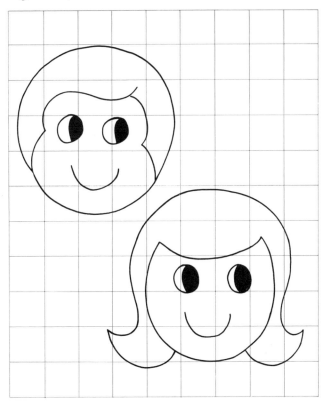

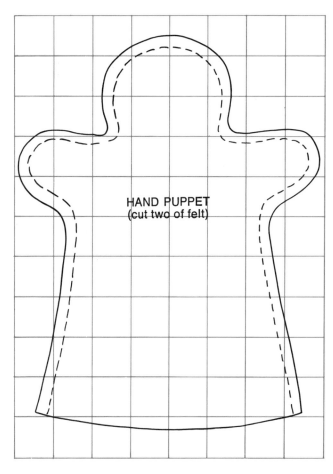

HAND PUPPET
(cut two of felt)

Figure 26
Hand puppet (enlarge to fit a 1" grid)

Felt Finger Puppets
You will need the same type of materials as for hand
puppet. Cut out finger puppet according to pattern.
Glue or sew it together on dotted lines. Add face and
other features. (See Figure 27.)

Figure 27
Simple, felt finger puppets (actual size)

5
Children Enjoy
Using Puppets Too

Children not only enjoy watching puppets; they also want to use and play with puppets themselves. And why shouldn't they, since working with puppets can be a constructive learning experience besides just plain fun.

Of course, you will need to give boys and girls some basic instructions on how to handle puppets. Discuss with them what is acceptable and unacceptable conduct when using puppets. Some children have a tendency to attack each other's puppets and pretend they are fighting or biting each other. In order to counteract this, discuss the kinds of behavior expected of people.

Do we get acquainted by biting each other? Of course not. We say "Hi," shake hands, or speak politely to each other. These are the kinds of things we can make our puppets do too. Talking about several types of behavior will help children think of a variety of actions for their puppets.

A group of second graders were given puppets as part of their language lesson. First, the teacher discussed ways of moving puppets to show happiness, sadness, shyness, etc. When the children tried out puppets themselves, they thought of other actions and expressions to illustrate many feelings and attitudes. One girl made her puppet act sleepy. Another child had the puppet behave as if it were eating something sour. One boy made the corners of the puppet's mouth turn down so that it looked angry.

In the school classroom, puppets can help children develop the ability to think creatively. As they invent characters and write stories or puppet skits, they learn to think from another's viewpoint and increase their understanding of other people and of the world in general.

Their stories can have true-life themes or pretend.

Figure 28
Children playing with puppets.

With a mouse puppet, children can imagine what a mouse sees or feels. What is it like to live inside a wall? How big does a flower look to a mouse?

If the mouse puppet is large, perhaps as large as the mice puppets, Teddy and Henry (see Figure 28), children may imagine what it would be like to be a big mouse. (It might be able to frighten the cat or chase the dog.) Under Teacher's direction, children may put together their ideas in the form of a skit and share it orally with the group, thus developing language skills.

When one of my daughters was in third grade, she and her friend made up a puppet skit which they presented to several classes. Their characters consisted of: a green monster (to represent a grassy lawn); a blue monster (to represent water); two orange monsters (to represent fire); a chicken (who was a doctor); and a boy (who represented the master).

In the first scene, the master told the water to take care of the lawn and see that it grew. The water agreed. But when the master left, the blue monster fell asleep instead.

The second scene showed the grass getting weaker and weaker. The fire brothers decided to take advantage of the weakening grass and burn it up. Just in time, the water woke up and chased the fire brothers away. The master came home in time to see what had happened. He was very angry and dismissed the water. He then called the doctor, who replanted the lawn.

Water begged to be allowed to do his job and the master agreed. The last scene showed everything going well. They decided to have a picnic, but someone forgot the rough time the lawn had had and sat on it.

Finding material to use in a puppet play can encourage children to be better readers. A third grade reading group used a story from their reading text as the basis for a puppet play. They wrote their own script, made their puppets, and practiced. Then they presented the play to the rest of the class, using an improvised stage.

These particular children were slow readers. Producing the play added immeasurably to their interest in reading and also boosted their flagging self-esteem. The rest of the class had the chance to develop good listening habits as they watched the others perform.

Using an existing story as the basis for a puppet script can be of value in still another way. It forces youngsters to pick out the most important parts of the story, rather than getting bogged down with details.

Puppets can be a part of the science curriculum. Rather than just reporting on various animals and their habits, children may present their reports, using animal puppets. A squirrel puppet can talk about what it does to get ready for winter or show how it gathers food.

As part of the social studies curriculum, puppets can be used to present problem situations which children face. A puppet skit on what it's like to be the new student in the class could be developed and given by the children. After the skit, the class could discuss attitudes and feelings of the newcomer. It could be especially effective if the newer students presented the skit, since their firsthand experience would make the activity more meaningful.

In the church program, time is often limited. Generally, children come to Sunday School a maximum of one hour a week. Much of the hour is used by the teacher giving the lesson. Extended amounts of free time are not usually available for children to use puppets themselves.

However, some of the activities already a part of classtime, such as review, could be adapted for puppets. Children could use puppets to act out the story as they review it.

The first time you let children use puppets in class, choose those who will set a good example for the others. When these children have used puppets successfully, others will want to take a turn. And when they can use puppets, shyer children will often take a more active part in Sunday School too.

Another possibility is to have children make their puppets one week and use them the following Sunday to review the story.

Younger children of kindergarten and nursery age often have a play period as part of the Sunday morning activities. Puppets can be a part of this playtime. When a child and teacher each have a puppet, they may be able to communicate better with each other. Children often feel more free to ask questions or to share their thoughts and feelings through a puppet.

During songtime, children can take turns leading with a puppet. Again, the puppet can help a shy child be more willing to get up in front of the group.

6
Writing Your Own Puppet Scripts

You probably realize—if you've checked with a Christian bookstore—that some books of puppet scripts are available (see page 71). However, you may not be able to find a script on the topic or theme you have in mind. So do consider writing your own script.

For plot ideas, you have inexhaustible resources. These include Bible stories, missionary stories, and life application stories found in books, Sunday School papers, and Bible curriculum. Children's literature, science and social studies books, and reading texts can provide materials for use in the school classroom.

Some stories are quite complicated and have many characters. In order to use these as puppet skits, you must simplify them. You can reduce many stories to three or four scenes, choosing only the most important parts to dramatize. Details that are necessary to the story but difficult to portray can be given by a narrator.

The Bible story of the Prodigal Son can be reduced to four basic scenes. The first scene would show the son asking his father for his share of the inheritance. The second scene would be the one in which the son is wasting his money with his friends until it is gone. The third scene would show the boy sitting with the pigs, deciding to go back home. The final one would show his return to his father's house. As many as six or seven puppets could be involved.

Or this story could be presented in four scenes with only two puppets; the boy and the father. Instead of having extra puppets for the boy's friends and the pigs, they could be drawn on the backgrounds.

Figure 29
A scene from "The Prodigal Son"

33

A traditional story such as "Goldilocks and the Three Bears" could also be presented in four scenes. In the first, the bears decide to take a walk. In the second, Goldilocks comes in and, after testing the chairs, the porridge, and the beds, falls asleep. In scene three, the bears come home and find that someone has been in their house. The final scene shows Goldilocks running away.

Dialogue can be expanded or kept to a minimum. If a narrator tells the story, there need be little or no conversation between the puppets. They may simply act out their parts as the story unfolds.

Children themselves provide a constant source of material for you to develop into scripts for puppets. The key to obtaining this material is observation. But be sure you watch an individual long enough to get a fair idea of his situation.

For instance, a child who might at first glance seem disruptive in a classroom may simply be more outgoing than the others and so become the scapegoat of the group. You want to be fair and realistic if you translate his situation into a skit so children will find the skit a fair picture of their experience.

If you teach Sunday School or work in other church-related programs, you may not have time to observe each child. Do consider other means of getting to know them better, such as visiting your students in their homes. Though a child may appear shy when "teacher" steps into his home, he will be delighted. And the insights you will gain from seeing his home situation will prove invaluable to you as you plan lessons and write skits for your puppets, not to mention the rapport such a contact can establish.

Whether you are observing in the classroom or at home, watch what children do and say. What kinds of things make them happy? What are their fears? What kinds of problems do they have getting along with playmates, parents, brothers and sisters? What kinds of sins give them the most trouble?

No doubt you have observed that children are often jealous of each other. The following skit, "The Bicycle Incident," illustrates jealousy and was developed after observing children in a home situation.

THE BICYCLE INCIDENT

Characters: Teddy, Henry, and Toby Turtle
TEDDY: Henry, you know what?
HENRY: What, Teddy?
TEDDY: I hate Toby!
HENRY: You what?
TEDDY: I hate Toby because he got a bicycle and he can't even ride it. It's not fair, Henry. I should have the bicycle.
HENRY: Where did Toby get the bicycle?
TEDDY: Larney Lion gave it to him. He should have given it to me, not Toby.

HENRY: Why, Teddy, I think you're jealous.
TEDDY: I am not! I just hate Toby.
HENRY: That's awful, Teddy. Hating and being jealous are wrong. Why, I bet if you asked Toby, he'd let you ride his bicycle.
TEDDY: No, he wouldn't. He's too selfish!
KNOCK! KNOCK! (Henry goes to answer the door and returns with Toby Turtle.)
TOBY: Hi Henry. Is Teddy here? I thought maybe he would like to ride my new bicycle. I don't know how to ride it yet. Maybe he could teach me how.
HENRY: Teddy, did you hear that?
TEDDY: Yes. I guess I was wrong to be jealous. Toby, I'd like to help you learn to ride your bicycle.
TOBY: All right. But you ride first so I can see how you do it.
(Toby and Teddy leave together.)
HENRY: Jealousy sure is bad! I'm glad they're friends again.

Figure 30
Teddy, Toby and Henry in "The Bicycle Incident"

You may want to present a puppet skit strictly for the fun of it. A puppet comedy routine can be extremely funny. And humor can be developed through a variety of means. One way is to have a puppet do or say someing unexpected. For instance, you offer the puppet a wrapped candy bar. Make it appear that he really wants it. He asks you to unwrap it so he can take a bite. You do so. Instead of biting the candy, he eats the wrapper or he bites you.

You'll also get laughs through the use of exaggeration. For example, the puppet may sneeze, but it is not an ordinary sneeze. He builds up to it. The audience will expect his sneeze to end with a final achoo! Instead, he does one of several things:

1. A-a-a-a-a-choo! (His hat or eyeglasses fall off.)
2. A-a-a-a-a-a (puppet speaks or sings and audience almost thinks he won't complete his sneeze. Then, unexpectedly, he does.)

3. He sneezes so loudly that the puppet stage or curtains and backgrounds shake, accompanied with crashing sounds.

Also, puppets can tell jokes or riddles. At camp, puppets were used in the evening funtime to tell about things that had actually happened during the camp day. Of course, the stories were slightly exaggerated, but the people who were the subjects of the jokes took it in good fun and even enjoyed being mentioned.

"The Earthquake" is a sample of the kind of skit given at camp.

THE EARTHQUAKE

Characters: Henry and Teddy Turtle
HENRY: Hey, Teddy, how was your first night at camp?
TEDDY: Terrible! I hardly got any sleep at all.
HENRY: Why not?
TEDDY: Well, I decided to sleep under a tree near rooms 11 and 12. In the middle of the night, the ground started to shake and—and—
HENRY: Go on—go on! What was it?
TEDDY: I thought it was an earthquake at first. Then I thought a bulldozer was coming.
HENRY: Well, what was it?
TEDDY: I finally looked into the window of rooms 11 12 and guess what?
HENRY: What?
TEDDY: Those kids were snoring like crazy. But, Henry—
HENRY: Yes, Teddy?
TEDDY: I didn't know little kids like that snored. I thought only counselors snored.
HENRY: I guess anyone snores if conditions are right.
TEDDY: Conditions sure must have been right last night.

When you use humor with your puppets, keep it apart from actual Bible stories or the serious part of a life-application story. Used inappropriately, humor can greatly damage your credibility when teaching a spiritual truth.

And be sure to keep the dialogue simple. Lengthy speaking parts will cause your audience to lose interest. It's also important to plan as much motion or activity for the puppets as possible. Since the puppets are not able to produce the wide variety of movements human actors can, you must make good use of the actions and motions they are capable of producing.

The way you write your script can help you. Here's one way: Make two columns on your paper. In the left-hand column, place the action to be produced next to the puppet's name. In the right-hand column, write the character's speaking part. This forces you to think beforehand of the action and helps you avoid holding a puppet in a lifeless position when it is speaking.

Here is an example using an excerpt from the preceding dialogue:

Action

HENRY: Leans toward Teddy.
TEDDY: Shakes head back and forth.
HENRY: Tips head.
TEDDY: Moves head around while speaking.

HENRY: Leans forward.
TEDDY: Jerks head up.

Speech

Hey, Teddy, how was your first night at camp?
Terrible! I hardly got any sleep at all.
Why not?
Well, I decided to sleep under a tree near rooms 11 and 12. In the middle of the night, the ground started to shake and—and—
Go on—go on! What was it?
I thought it was an earthquake at first. Then I thought a bulldozer was coming.

It's usually best to keep your puppet play short. If it is a long story, break it up into three or four scenes. This will keep the action moving and hold the audience's attention.

So there you have it. You may find some good commercially prepared puppet scripts. However, your own observations and research can enable you to produce some good material too—if you apply these rules in constructing your scripts: Add humor; keep scripts simple and short; consider the action; and make practical, spiritual applications.

7
How To
Stage a Puppet Play

If you teach or work with very young children, you won't be staging a puppet play. Your skits will be short and informal. However, if you work with older children, you may want to stage some puppet presentations.

The kind of staging you use, whether for a school classroom, Sunday School, or more formal presentations, needn't be expensive or complicated.

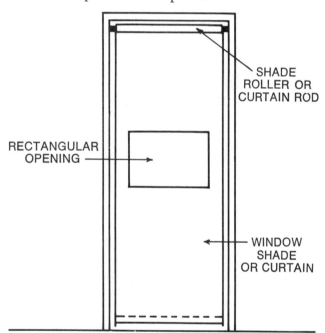

Figure 31
Curtain or window shade stage

Window Shade or Curtain Stage
One of the simplest ways of making a puppet stage is to purchase a spring-tension curtain rod to fit a doorway. Make the curtain of vinyl upholstery fabric. Cut a rectangular opening in the curtain at a height that

will allow the puppeteers to kneel, sit, or stand to operate their puppets.

If you want a stage that is easy to store, purchase a window shade and have it cut to fit inside your doorway. Attach the vinyl curtain to the window shade roller after removing the original shade. (You may be able to purchase a shade made of opaque material heavy enough for your purpose.) There are two advantages to this type of shade-stage: When you are not using the "stage," you may simply roll it up. And you can adjust the shade level so the opening is at a suitable height for any puppeteers.

Figure 32
Puppet stage made from a large appliance box

Packing Box or Appliance Box Stage

Another simple, inexpensive stage can be made from a large packing box (see Figure 32). You should be able to get one of these from a large department store warehouse, free of charge. The box can be painted and decorated by the teacher or children. Inexpensive poster paints or other water base paints work well on heavy cardboard.

The box may be used to provide either a four-sided, closed-in stage, or one side can be cut open to provide a double-width, three-sided stage.

Directions for Making an Appliance Box Stage

Materials needed (for either a three or four-sided stage):
- One large appliance box
- Tape (if the box has been cut open on one side)
- Water-base paint
- Dowel rod, ½″ or 1″ thick and 4″ longer than width of box. One needed for four-sided stage, two,for three-sided stage.
- Fabric for draw curtains that is soft and opaque
- Large sheets of paper or cloth for backdrop on three-sided stage

Tools Needed:
- Sharp knife or linoleum cutter
- Saw
- Paintbrushes

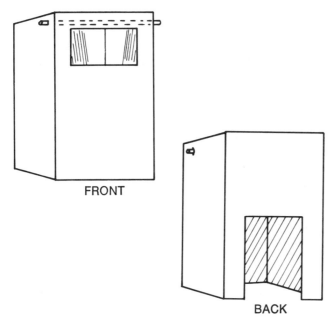

Figure 33
A four-sided appliance box stage

Model 1: A Four-sided Stage

Cut the closing flaps from the top and bottom of the box. If the box has been cut open on one side, tape the side shut. Remove any loose staples or other sharp objects which could scratch or injure children. Stand the box upright. Cut an opening in the lower half of

the box. Be sure it is large enough for a puppeteer to crawl through. Leave the upper part intact so that backgrounds may be fastened to the inside of it. This area will form the back of the puppet stage.

Cut an opening in the upper half of the front of the box at a height which will be comfortable for the children to hold their puppets when kneeling.

Cut two round holes, slightly bigger than the dowel rod, about four inches from the front of the stage on both sides of the box. The stage curtains will be hung on the dowel and placed here.

Hem the sides of the two curtain panels (be sure these panels will cover the stage opening when drawn together). Then hem the tops and bottoms. Make the top hem large enough so that the dowel rod will pass through it easily and the curtains can be drawn back and forth.

Paint and decorate the stage as desired. Then thread the curtains on the dowel rod and insert the dowel ends into the holes cut in the sides of the box.

Model 2: A Three-sided Stage

Open one side of the box if it is not already open. Cut off the top and bottom closing flaps. Remove loose staples or other sharp objects. Spread the box open to form a double-width front and two single-width sides. Cut an opening for the stage in the center of the upper half of the front (see Figure 34).

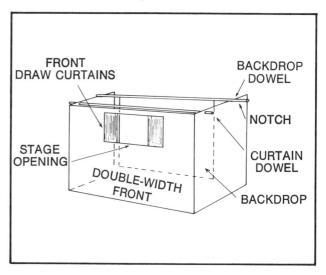

Figure 34
A three-sided appliance box stage

Cut two notches slightly bigger than the dowel rod about four inches from the back of the stage on the sides of the box. Make the backdrop of material and fasten it to the second dowel and place dowel ends in the two notches. Or make up a variety of paper backgrounds with different scenes. Attach each scene to a rod with masking tape, and use the appropriate scene when staging your play. Follow the same instructions for curtain and rod, given for the four-sided stage. Paint stage as desired.

FRONT

BACK AND SIDE

Figure 35
Plywood stage

Portable Plywood Stage

This stage is constructed so that it can be taken apart and stored or transported easily.

Materials needed:
- Two 64″ x 24″ pieces of ¼″ plywood
- Two 64″ x 48″ pieces of ¼″ plywood
- Three 5′ lengths of 1″ x 2″ boards
- Six removable pin hinges
- Four small gate hooks and eyes
- One yard of 45″ fabric for backdrop
- One traverse rod for front curtains
- One pair of curtains for front opening
- Paint

Diagrams and instructions for constructing this puppet stage are found in Figures 36 and 37.

Panel Stage

The diagrams given in the following pages provide directions for constructing a four-panel stage (see Figure 42) which can be used to stage a formal or informal puppet presentation. It can be taken apart in less than 10 minutes. The stage features cloth side-curtains and a cloth backdrop. The setting for your puppet play or skit can be changed by painting different scenes on different cloth backgrounds with acrylic paints.

An optional side window is included in the plans. You may operate a puppet by yourself by standing outside the stage and running your arm through the side opening with the puppet on your hand. This enables you to carry on a one-person puppet dialogue.

Front draw curtains and lights may be added if desired. If you intend to have a lighted puppet stage, be sure to attach lights below and above the stage opening. If you provide lighting from the top or bottom only, the resulting shadows may detract from your puppet performance.

If you install lights, be sure to take these special precautions: Always use lamps that are UL approved. And do use lights that give off as little heat as possible. Also use protective covers. These should be made of a material which will not overheat and burn a puppeteer who may come in contact with them. And the covers should be fireproof.

Do not drive nails or staples through electrical cords which are attached to the lights. (Shocks may result.) And keep electrical cords out of the area where puppeteers must sit or kneel, so that their feet and legs do not become entangled.

This puppet stage has been designed so that it can be taken apart by pulling the pins from the hinges and unhooking the gate hooks. When you use prefinished

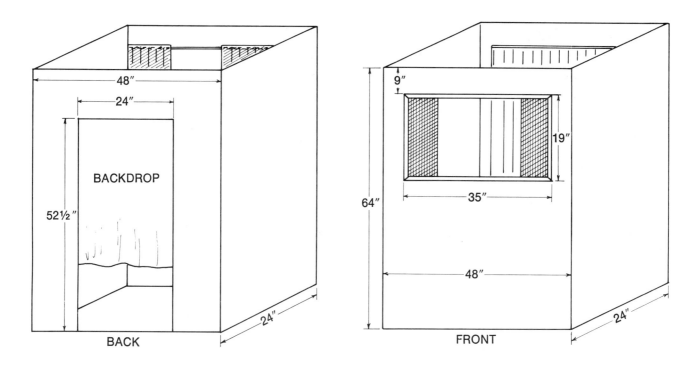

Figure 36
Portable, plywood puppet stage (outside)

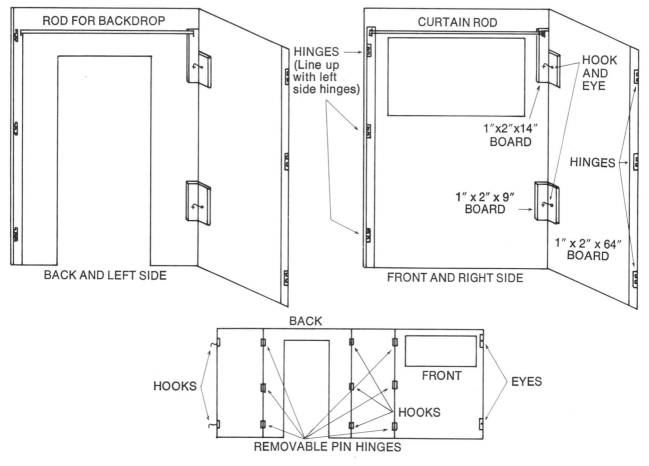

Figure 37
Portable, plywood puppet stage (inside)

paneling, you don't even need to paint your stage.

The following pages (Figures 38 to 41) show how to make the Panel Stage.

Impromptu Staging

If you lack time, materials, or skill, but still want some type of simple stage setting, consider these possibilities: Use a table, turned on its side or draped with a cloth or sheet. Setting it in front of a blank wall will provide you with a plain background. You or the children can paint an appropriate scene on a large sheet of paper and put it on the wall behind your "stage."

You can even use a low spinet piano. A tall one is not recommended for children, since most boys and girls would have to stand on chairs in order to reach over the top. As a general safety rule, it is best to use a stage that children may kneel, sit, or stand behind, rather than one that would require them to stand on chairs, since they could easily lose their balance while holding puppets over their heads.

Children may even improvise a stage, using the back of a chair or couch. They could simply kneel behind it and hold their puppets up over the back.

Whatever type of staging you choose, you will find that it can enhance your puppet performance and make children puppeteers feel like pros. However, when beginning to work with puppets, it is the best to keep things simple and easy to handle so neither you nor the children who work with you become discouraged and miss the fun of a puppet production.

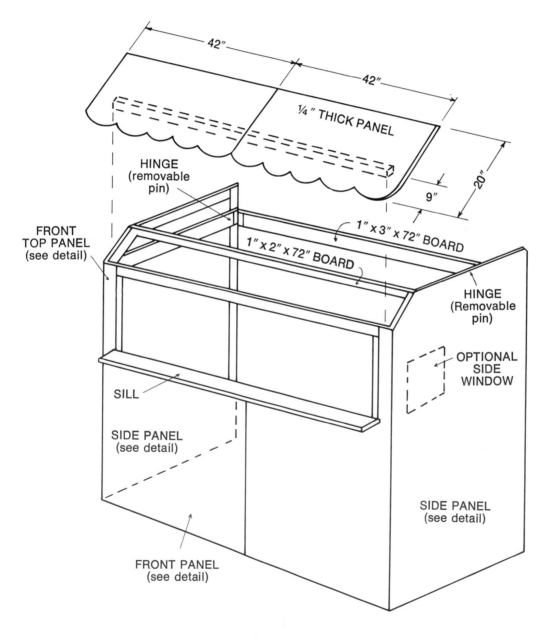

Figure 38
Panel stage (outside front)

40

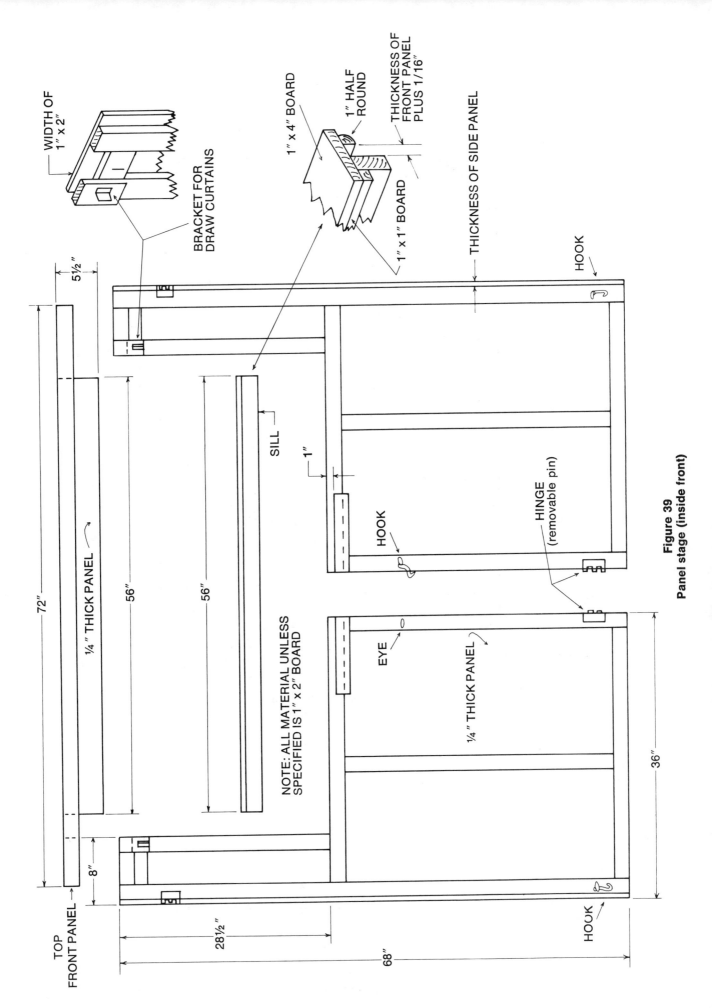

WIDTH OF 1" x 2"

BRACKET FOR DRAW CURTAINS

1" x 4" BOARD

1" HALF ROUND

THICKNESS OF FRONT PANEL PLUS 1/16"

1" x 1" BOARD

THICKNESS OF SIDE PANEL

HOOK

5½"

¼" THICK PANEL

56"

SILL

1"

HOOK

72"

HINGE (removable pin)

EYE

¼" THICK PANEL

56"

NOTE: ALL MATERIAL UNLESS SPECIFIED IS 1" x 2" BOARD

36"

TOP FRONT PANEL

8"

28½"

HOOK

68"

Figure 39
Panel stage (inside front)

41

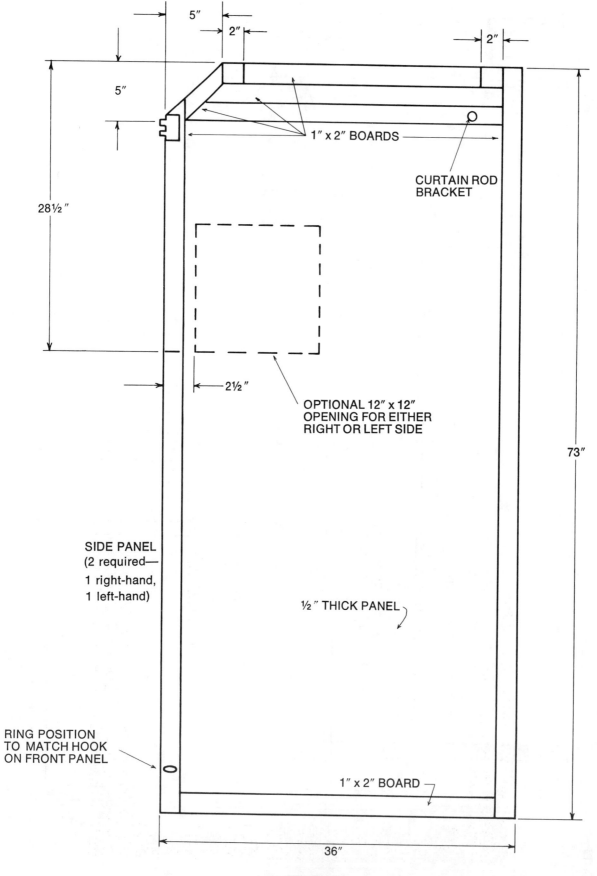

Figure 40
Panel stage (inside sideview)

42

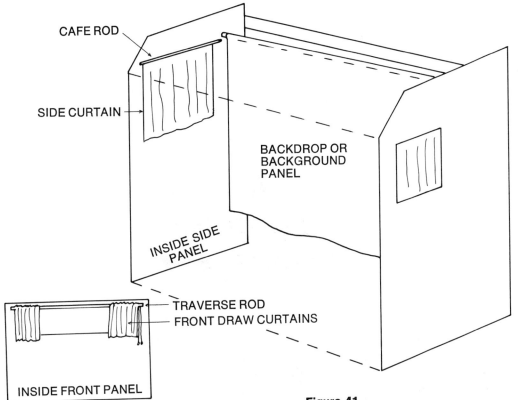

CAFE ROD

SIDE CURTAIN

BACKDROP OR
BACKGROUND
PANEL

INSIDE SIDE
PANEL

TRAVERSE ROD
FRONT DRAW CURTAINS

INSIDE FRONT PANEL

Figure 41
Panel stage showing position of curtains

Figure 42
A finished panel stage in use

43

8
Organizing a Puppet Team

An important goal of a church or other organization is to reach and interest people in its work or ministry. A puppet team can have a twofold effect in this respect. First of all, the puppet team members benefit by learning how to speak before groups of people. They also learn how to promote their organization and in so doing develop a loyalty to it. Secondly, when the church or school puppet team performs well, people are attracted to the work of the school or church represented.

For example, a church puppet team might obtain permission to set up a booth at a local shopping center or fair. They could schedule performances every 15 to 30 minutes, depending on the length of the production. Members of the team could use the time in between performances to talk to passersby, or give out tracts or other promotional materials.

The actual content of the puppet play or skit could have either a teaching or promotional message. Here is a skit idea for promoting Vacation Bible School, called "Our Secret."

OUR SECRET

Characters: Hoby Hippo and Larney Lion

HOBY   (On stage as scene opens): I wonder where Larney Lion is. Larney! *Oh, Larney!*

LARNEY   (Rushing onstage): Hoby, whatever is the matter? I thought you were hurt or something.

HOBY: No, I was just lonely. Where is everyone? I went to Marty Monkey's house and Gerry Giraffe's and—

LARNEY: —and they weren't home?

HOBY: Well, no one answered when I knocked. Where do you think they are, Larney?

LARNEY: I think they're getting ready.

HOBY: For what?

LARNEY: Can you keep a secret?

HOBY: Sure. What is it?

(Larney whispers something in Hoby's ear.)

HOBY: Really? But why are you whispering good news like that?

LARNEY: Oh, I just pretended it was a secret so you'd get excited about it. I know you can't keep a secret and if I tell you it's a secret then you'll tell everyone.

HOBY: I don't get it.

LARNEY: Never mind. Just tell them our secret.

HOBY: Nope! I don't tell secrets.

LARNEY: But you're supposed to tell this one. Now go on and tell them.

HOBY   (Whispering): _____Church is having Vacation Bible Bible School_____to _____and Larney and I will be there.

LARNEY: Hoby—

HOBY: What Larney? Did I say it wrong?

LARNEY: No, silly. You said it right but you didn't say it loud enough.

HOBY: But isn't it a secret?

LARNEY: No, not really. C'mon now I'm having trouble keeping my patience.

HOBY: I didn't know you were a doctor!

LARNEY: Cut that out, Hoby. Tell them again about Vacation Bible School. This time say it LOUD!

HOBY   (Loudly): OK, here goes. _____Church is having Vacation Bible School_____ to_____and Larney and I will be there!

LARNEY: That's better. Now tell them who is invited.

HOBY   (Croaking): You tell them. All that yelling made me hoarse.

LARNEY: It's for children, ages_____through
_____. It starts at_____o'clock
and lasts until_____o'clock, Monday
through Friday.
HOBY: What kinds of things do people do at Bible
School?
LARNEY: There'll be songs, stories, refreshments,
games, crafts, and (Hoby starts to leave)
Where are you going, Hoby?
HOBY: I'm goin' home to get all my work done so
I'll be ready for Vacation Bible School.
LARNEY: Good thinking, Hoby. See you later. (Turns
to audience) I hope we'll see all of you there
too.

This skit could also be used to promote Vacation Bible School in the various departments of the Sunday School itself. Or it could be presented in a church service or any other church-related agency.

If you have an interest in sponsoring a puppet team, decide what age group will be involved. Sometimes this will be determined for you by the interests of the young people themselves or simply the availability of people.

You may find young people from fourth grade through high school who are interested in joining a puppet team. Even college-age young people may be interested in participating or being sponsors. If the response is good and young people in several age groups are interested, you can divide the groups up according to ages and get sponsors to work with each group.

Even if only two or three youngsters of varying ages show an interest in forming a puppet team, you should not be discouraged. These few can be the core group of your team. As they begin to perform and become known, others may be influenced to join the team.

In starting a puppet team, it is important to plan for success no matter how large or small the group is or what ages the children are. Don't expose the group to failure by starting out the wrong way.

One wrong way is to expect your young people to begin by making their own puppets and writing their own scripts. If children try to make their own puppets, they may get bogged down and lose interest in giving a play or skit, simply because their puppets are not as nice as they expected them to be.

At first, obtain some attractive, ready-made puppets. And use a prepared script. It should be simple, requiring a minimum of speaking and staging. Practice the skit or play as often as necessary to have it go smoothly. But don't overpractice, or the youngsters may lose interest.

When the group is ready, share the production with a small group at your church, school, or agency. It's important that the first few performances be presented before audiences that will be very supportive. When children perform before other children, you might have them present their play for a group younger than themselves rather than for children who are older. Generally a younger audience will look up to older children and be more appreciative and lend more moral support to the team.

Figure 43
A puppet team, ready to go

Use those first performances as good publicity or advertisement for the puppet team. After the presentation, the sponsor can invite those who are interested in working with puppets to join the team. Mention meeting times and places so that children will know exactly how to join the group. Youngsters who don't attend church and Sunday School regularly may be challenged by the opportunity to become a part of a puppet team. Children who are somewhat shy about speaking before a group may be willing members of a puppet team, since they do not have to be seen by the audience.

As the group grows, find out which children work best together and allow them to work as subteams. Since most skits require a maximum of three people for their production, several small groups could be working on different skits. If the group is mixed in age, provide both simple and complex materials so that each person may experience success and also be challenged.

After you have a good-sized puppet team which is experienced and confident, you may have them try writing their own scripts and making their own puppets. At this point, they may also want to make backgrounds and other stage properties. A puppet team at a Christian school in Phoenix, Arizona works on their presentation for several months. Then they invite the rest of the school and the parents to their performance.

Appreciative audiences can be found in many places. In a day school, other classes may be the audience. If the group members are very accomplished puppeteers, they may wish to perform in a school assembly or Christian school chapel service. In a church situation, a puppet team may perform for almost any service, weekday club, or special group. Bus rallies and holiday programs may also feature puppets.

A puppet team may find outlets for their talents outside the school or church. Rest homes often welcome outsiders coming in to cheer their residents. Many older people are delighted to have contact with young people and children. A puppet team can present a Bible story or life application story and, in this way, minister to old or young.

Another place which might welcome puppeteers is a children's ward in a hospital. Several people have related instances in which children, who had undergone surgery or were seriously ill, responded better to puppets than to human visitors. Their recovery was actually hastened because they had renewed interest in life.

In the church, school, and community, a puppet team can effectively minister to the needs of others, while at the same time developing the skills and talents of its own members. Furthermore the puppet team can be a good advertisement for the larger group it represents.

9
Puppet Scripts You Can Use

The scripts in the first section of this chapter cover a variety of subjects and are listed according to length with the shortest, simplest ones first. All may be used with several different applications. However, only one application is supplied, and it may or may not be the one you should use with your particular group.

If the application is too mature for your preschoolers, for instance, use the skit and develop your own application. Or let the skit itself be the application for a Bible story or conduct lesson you're teaching.

Bible references are also supplied. Again, these may fit your group and your teaching situation or they may not. Do be selective. Some verses will not be appropriate for the very young. Others will. So consider all you know about the particular age group you are working with as you select the scripts, applications, and verses.

The script series called "Monsters in Our Lives" appears toward the end of the chapter. This is a group of five lessons, written for children in grades three to six. Each lesson is introduced with a short puppet dialogue. The puppets for these may be made by following instructions in Chapter Four for the shaggy dog or monster puppet. Special features for each monster are included at the beginning of the set of lessons. Other scripts in this book also incorporate the use of monsters.

1. HOBY FEELS SORRY FOR HIMSELF

Theme: Self-concept
Characters: Hoby Hippo* and the teacher
Setting: None

TEACHER   (Holds Hoby behind back): Hoby, are you there?

HOBY   (comes out hesitantly, sobbing): Boohoo! Boohoo!

TEACHER: What's wrong, Hoby?

HOBY   (Shakes head): Oh, nothing. Sob, sob!

TEACHER: Then why are you crying?

HOBY   (Nods): It's just everything. I'm fat and dumb, and no one likes me.

TEACHER   (Shakes head): Hoby, that's not true. We all like you. You're special!

HOBY   (Shakes head): 'Specially fat and dumb!

*Larney Lion, Hoby Hippo, Reggie (Reginald) Rabbit, Suzy Squirrel, Peggy Panda, and Lester Lamb may be purchased from Scripture Press Publications; Wheaton, Ill. 60187 or from your local Christian bookstore. The other puppets mentioned may be obtained from Puppets by Shelly; Phoenix, Arizona 85018.

TEACHER: Now stop that! You have extra special good things about you that no one else has.

HOBY   (Shakes head): I can't think of any! Boohoo, boohoo!

TEACHER: Hoby, I know you swim very well. Didn't you rescue a monkey from drowning?

HOBY   (Nods): Y-y-yes, I did that. (Sniffles)

TEACHER: See, you can do something well. Don't you feel better?

HOBY   (Looks at teacher): A little. I'll have to think about it. I better go now. See you later.

TEACHER: 'Bye, Hoby.

POSSIBLE APPLICATION: Sometimes people feel sorry for themselves just as Hoby did. They don't think they're good at anything. But God has made each of us for a special purpose. He loves each of us so much that he sent His Son, Jesus, to die for our sins. He wants everyone of us to ask Jesus to be our Saviour. And He has a home in heaven for everyone who does.

When we ask Jesus to be our Saviour, He forgives our sin and gives us happiness and joy. He also has a special job for each of us to do for Him. Everyone has some talent he can use for God—to honor Him. We can use our voices to sing praises to Him and tell others about His love. We can run errands, be friendly, helpful, or cheer those who are lonely or sick. Perhaps you can think of other ways you can serve Him.

BIBLE VERSES: Rom. 12:1-2; James 4:10; Mark 12:31; Matt. 25:40; Eph. 2:8-10. BIBLE STORIES: Esther; Paul's conversion and service in Acts 8—28

2. HOBY'S LOST JACKET

Theme: Self-control, courtesy, responsibility, patience
Characters: Hoby Hippo and Larney Lion
Setting: A living room

HOBY   (Comes in looking all around as if he has lost something): Larney, have you seen my jacket?

LARNEY   (in the corner looking out the window; turns to look at Hoby): I'm sorry, Hoby. I haven't seen it lately.

HOBY   (Moves around here and there; speaks impatiently, each sentence louder than the previous one): Oh, this makes me mad! I want my jacket! Well, why don't you help me find it?

LARNEY   (Moves to where Hoby is): Why are you so angry? I didn't take your jacket.

HOBY   (Moves as if jumping up and down): I need my jacket!

LARNEY: Why are you shouting? It won't help you find your jacket.

HOBY   (Mouth wide open, shouting): THEN WHY DON'T YOU HELP ME?!

LARNEY: Why don't you ask me nicely?

HOBY   (Shakes and shouts): HELP ME FIND IT!!

LARNEY: Only if you calm down.

HOBY   (Paces back and forth as if trying to calm down): U-u-u-u-u-u-u-h-h!! (clear throat and stops beside Larney and speaks quietly) Larney?

LARNEY (Tips head to one side): Yes, Hoby?

HOBY (Head down): Would you please help me find my jacket?

LARNEY   (Nods): Sure, Hoby. I'd be happy to help you. You look in the bedroom, and I'll look in the kitchen.

(Hoby and Larney leave in opposite directions.)

POSSIBLE APPLICATION: Hoby needs to learn that taking care of his jacket is his responsibility. Have you ever lost something and then gotten mad because you couldn't find it? I have. Sometimes we even blame other people and make them feel bad when it isn't their fault.

God can help us learn to be patient with others and be responsible for our own things. First we need to ask Him to be our Saviour if we never have before. Then He will always be with us. He will help us not to get mad when we misplace something if we ask for His help. He'll help us remember to be kind and courteous to other people. But we must let Him help us. Here are some verses from the Bible that tell us to be patient.

BIBLE VERSES: Eph. 4:32; Prov. 16:32a

3. LET'S HAVE A LITTLE COOPERATION AROUND HERE

Theme: Cooperation
Characters: Teacher; two boy puppets—Billy and Bobby; two girl puppets—Polly and Patty
Setting: Living room or plain background

TEACHER (To audience): Today some of our puppet friends are going to teach us a new song. Before they sing, I'd like to introduce them to you. (To puppets): All right, in there; are you ready to sing for us?

(Puppets do not come out and curtain remains closed. Only their voices are heard.)

BILLY: No, not that song. I won't sing that one you picked.

POLLY: Well, I'm certainly not going to sing the one YOU picked!

BOBBY: If you asked me, I don't want to sing at all.

TEACHER (Knocks on puppet stage): Hey, what's going on in there? Open these curtains right now! (Curtain opens. Puppets are still hidden.)

BOBBY (Comes out and looks back toward the others): Ouch! He just hit me with a book!

BILLY (Moves quickly toward Bobby): I did not. It fell off the shelf, and you were in the way!

POLLY (Joins the others on stage): I saw the whole thing and Bobby asked for it. He said he wouldn't even sing with us.

PATTY (Joins the others): Well, I don't blame him. I won't either!

TEACHER: Now stop your arguing. I want you to line up here this minute!

(Puppets all argue and talk at once.)

TEACHER: Did you hear me? ATTENTION!

(Puppets all stop talking and stand still.)

TEACHER: That's better. Now what is this all about?

(Puppets all talk at once.)

TEACHER (Holds up hand at them): Hold it! One at a time. Billy, you tell me what this fight is all about.

BILLY (Moves head around): Well, I didn't want to sing the song they picked.

POLLY (Moves forward): And we didn't like the one HE chose.

PATTY and BOBBY (Together): Yeah!

TEACHER: I'm sure there is some way of settling this without fighting. You were supposed to be good examples to these children. Aren't you ashamed?

(Puppets all hang their heads.)

49

BILLY   (Looks up slightly): I'm sorry.

ALL OTHERS   (Look up slowly): We're sorry.

TEACHER: Well, that's better. Now let's decide what song you're going to sing. Which one do you all like?

BOBBY: I like (names the song you have chosen for your children to learn).

POLLY and PATTY   (Together): I like that song.

BILLY   (Nods): Well, it's not my favorite but it's OK.

TEACHER: Good! Let's hear you sing.
(Either have the puppets sing the song together or play a recording of the song you've chosen.)

TEACHER   (To puppets): That was very nice. (To children): Did you boys and girls notice how good they sounded when they worked together? It helps to cooperate. (To puppets): How about singing that once more and then we'll sing with you.

PUPPETS   (All nod): OK. (They sing again.)

BILLY   (To teacher and children): Hey, I'm starting to like that song. Maybe all of you could sing with us now.

(Everyone sings.)

POSSIBLE APPLICATION: When we fight among ourselves, nothing gets done. God wants us to learn to do our part cheerfully. When Christian boys and girls fight among themselves, it looks bad to those who are not yet Christians.

BIBLE VERSE: James 3:16

4. HOBY'S DISCOVERY

Theme: Honesty
Characters: Hoby Hippo and Larney Lion
Setting: Outdoor scene

Props: Pictures of Hoby's dream foods enlarged from small drawings, using a 1″-grid (Figure 44) and mounted on cardboard. Attach each picture to a stick so it can be held up by a puppeteer at the appropriate time. Or tie a strong nylon thread to the top of each picture and hang the thread over some crosspiece at the top of your stage. Attach the other end of the thread to a stick so puppeteers may lower each drawing from the top at the right moment. The puppeteer should be hidden behind the backdrop.

HOBY   (Leaning over and moving head back and forth as if counting money from a wallet he has just found): Boy, there's a lot of money here! Eight, nine, ten . . . I'm sure glad I found this. Just think of all the things I can buy with it. What will I buy first? Now let's see—what are my favorite things?
(Puppeteer holds up picture of Hoby eating a banana split.)

HOBY   (Nods): Yeah, a banana split. Yummy! With all this money I can get a super big one.
(Puppeteer removes banana split and holds up picture of Hoby drinking a huge root beer float.)

HOBY   (Looks up): Maybe I should get a giant root beer float—the biggest one ever made—or—
(Puppeteer removes float and replaces it with a picture of Hoby in a field of donuts.)

HOBY   (Looking around): Maybe I could buy dozens of donuts—or—
(Puppeteer removes picture of donuts and replaces it with one of a giant candy bar.)

HOBY   (Nods): That's it! A gigantic candy bar, all fudgy with nuts in it and gooey caramel and—
(Puppeteer removes picture of candy.)

50

HOBY: Oh, I can't wait to spend MY money!

LARNEY (Comes in and acts surprised): Hoby, where did you get all that money? You didn't steal it, did you?

HOBY (Shakes head): No. Larney, honest I didn't. I-I found it. Really, I did.

LARNEY: Where did you find it?

HOBY (Looks down): It was in that wallet. I found it on the sidewalk in front of the ice-cream store.

LARNEY: Well, did you go into the store and ask if anyone lost it?

HOBY (Shakes head): No, I never thought of that.

LARNEY (Looks at Hoby, then down): Well, you should have. Just think, Hoby, someone may be looking for that wallet right now.

HOBY (Hangs head and sniffles): I guess you're right.

LARNEY (Comes over to Hoby and nudges him): Don't cry about it. Did you look in the wallet to see if there's a name in it?

HOBY (Keeps head down): No, I didn't think of it. You look, Larney.

LARNEY (Bends low as if looking down at wallet): Yes, here it is. It belongs to (choose a name).

HOBY: Is there an address too?

LARNEY (Nods excitedly): Yes, here it is.

HOBY: Let's take the wallet there now.
(Both puppets leave the scene. In a few moments, they return.)

HOBY (Bouncing): Boy, Larney, you sure are smart. I feel so good about giving that wallet back to _____.

LARNEY: So do I.

HOBY (Tilts head): Larney, did you know _____ would give us a reward?

LARNEY (Shakes head): No, I didn't, but it's always best to be honest, reward or no reward.

HOBY (Nods): Larney, what are you going to do with the reward money?

LARNEY (Looking up): We'll have to think about that for a while.

HOBY: I had some ideas before. Want to hear them?

LARNEY: I'm not sure about your ideas, Hoby.

POSSIBLE APPLICATION: Hoby said that it made him feel good to be honest, and that's true. Doing the right thing makes us feel good—most of the time. But more important, it pleases God—all of the time. God expects Christians to be honest in everything they do.

BIBLE VERSES: Rom. 12:17; 1 Thes. 4:12; Rom. 13:13

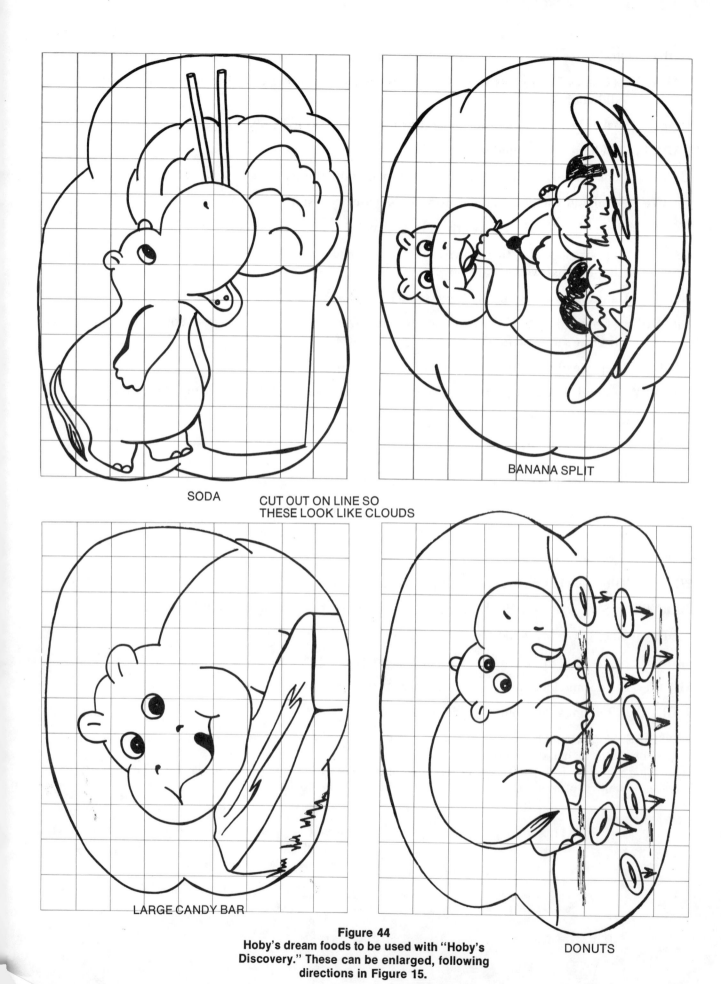

SODA

BANANA SPLIT

CUT OUT ON LINE SO
THESE LOOK LIKE CLOUDS

LARGE CANDY BAR

Figure 44
Hoby's dream foods to be used with "Hoby's
Discovery." These can be enlarged, following
directions in Figure 15.

DONUTS

Theme: Cheating, following rules, playing fairly
Characters: Hoby Hippo and Larney Lion
Setting: A living room. Larney and Hoby are playing checkers.

HOBY   (Shakes head while looking down): Oh, no! You jumped my man again!

LARNEY   (Tilts head to one side): King me!

HOBY   (Looking down): If you get another king, I won't have any checkers left.

LARNEY: C'mon. Let's play.

HOBY   (Shakes head): I'm sure not doing very well.

LARNEY   (Nods): Uh-huh!

HOBY   (Moves back and shakes head): Oh no! You jumped me again!

LARNEY: Sorry. You've got to think, Hoby. (Looks down)

HOBY   (Nods): I know. (Moves back and lifts head): Hey, Larney?

LARNEY   (Keeps head down): What?

HOBY (Leans toward Larney): I'm kind of hungry. Do you have any snacks?

LARNEY   (Looks up at Hoby): Oh, you're always hungry. I'll go get you something.

HOBY: (Bounces up and down as Larney leaves. When Larney is out of sight, he speaks and moves around as if changing checkers): Oh boy! Now's my chance. I'll just move these checkers around so I'll have a chance to win.

LARNEY   (Enters and bends down as if setting something down): Here's some crackers, Hoby. Come and get 'em.

HOBY   (Keeps head down): Never mind that now, Larney. Let's play checkers.

LARNEY   (Tips head and looks at Hoby): Well, I like that! I go to the trouble of getting you something to eat and now you don't want it.

HOBY: I'll have something later. Let's finish this game first. C'mon!

LARNEY   (Looks down, then up at Hoby): Hey, wait a minute, Hoby. What did you do to this checkerboard? (Moves excitedly up and down) Why, you rascal, you tried to cheat me. I ought to—

HOBY   (Shaking): I—I'm sorry, Larney. I—I—I just didn't want to lose again. Please don't hit me. Don't get angry!

LARNEY: Hoby, let me tell you something. When you play a game, you have rules. Rules help everyone who plays. If you don't follow the rules, why play?

HOBY   (Hangs head): But if we keep the rules, I always lose.

LARNEY   (Moves by Hoby as if to comfort him): But don't you see, Hoby, if you cheat, you're still a loser. Winning isn't really winning unless you win fair and square. Let's play again and I'll show you how to play better.

HOBY   (Nods): Oh, would you, Larney? Good! Now, I think I'll have those crackers.

POSSIBLE APPLICATION: It's fun to win a game, isn't it? And it's most fun when you win "fair and square." But sometimes it takes a lot of practice to become good enough to win at a game or sport. You may be tempted to take the cheating "shortcut."

If you do cheat, you cheat only yourself because you haven't really learned to do the thing well.

God has a lot to say in the Bible about being honest or not deceitful. He expects us to play and work fair. If we don't, we are sinning, and should confess our sin to Him (1 John 1:9). Then we should ask His forgiveness and help to be faithful in learning a task or skill or game well enough to be a good sport when we lose.

BIBLE VERSES: Ps. 101:7; Ps. 120:2; Prov. 12:5, 20; Ps. 119:118; Mark 7:20-22

6. WHAT IS CHRISTMAS?

> Characters: Two mice—Teddy and Henry; and Lester Lamb
>
> Setting: Living room (or plain white backdrop)

Props: Suede-Graph "Christmas" or a Christmas filmstrip and filmstrip projector set up behind the puppet stage so that strip can be projected on a plain backdrop at the back of the puppet stage. A small Christmas tree.

HENRY (Enters and jerks as if surprised): A-a-a-a-h! We've been robbed! Teddy, call the forest ranger! The game warden! Call anyone! Teddy!

TEDDY: Henry, did you call me! (Enters)

HENRY (Nods): Yes. Just look at this room! What happened to all our furniture?

TEDDY: Oh that; I moved it all out.

HENRY: Why did you do a crazy thing like that?

TEDDY: Stay right here, Henry, and I'll show you. (He leaves.)

HENRY (To audience): I wonder what he's up to now?

TEDDY (Enters, dragging the Christmas tree): Look, Henry! I got a Christmas tree.

HENRY (Moves back from tree): Teddy, if you set up that tree in here, there won't be any room for us.

TEDDY: That's all right, Henry. I don't mind if you move out.

HENRY: You're impossible!

TEDDY (Tilts head): No I'm not. I'm Teddy.

HENRY (Leans toward Teddy): Now cut that out, Teddy. Get that tree out of here or make it smaller so we can live here too.

TEDDY (Leaving with tree): OK. (Comes back without tree) Henry?

HENRY (Turns to look at Teddy): What now?

TEDDY (Tips head): What is Christmas?

HENRY (Tilts head): Well, it's giving gifts and—and well, everyone decorates his house and—and— (A knock is heard.) Oh! I'd better answer the door. (He turns to the corner as if to answer the door.) Oh, hi, Lester. C'mon in.

TEDDY (Moves toward Henry and Lester as they move to center stage): Hi, Lester. I'm sure glad it's you. Say, maybe you can answer my question.

LESTER: What is it, Teddy?

TEDDY (Tips head): Lester, what is Christmas?

LESTER (Excited): Oh, Christmas is a wonderful time!

HENRY AND TEDDY: But why?

LESTER: Because of the first Christmas. Some of my relatives were there long ago in a field outside Bethlehem with some shepherds. That's how I know. This is how the story goes:

(You may wish to tell the Christmas story yourself, using the *Christmas* Suede-Graph. You may even have the children sing appropriate Christmas songs in between scenes or have the music played on the piano or on records in the background.

Or you may wish to project from the rear of the puppet stage a Christmas filmstrip on a plain backdrop while a narrator reads the Bible story (unless you have a recording that goes with the filmstrip) or tells it in his own words.)

POSSIBLE APPLICATION: That very first Christmas, God sent us His Son—the very best Gift. Sadly, all people won't accept God's gift. They just won't believe that Jesus came to die to forgive their sins. I hope you love the Lord Jesus and believe in Him. If you do, then you have received God's very best Gift—Jesus Christ.

MONSTERS IN OUR LIVES

"Monsters in our Lives" is a set of five lessons for children junior age and up. Five problem areas are defined and described. They are anger, fear, worry, pride, and envy. The lessons point out the sinful aspects of these problems and can be used to help youngsters find God's answers.

A Bible drill and puppet skit introduce each problem. Suggestions for developing the lessons are also included. Chapter Three gives some ideas for presenting the monster skits. You may wish to put the puppets' speaking parts on tape and speak your part live or present the whole skit live by having your helper speak the monsters' parts.

For the Bible drill, you might tell the children that there is one key word in each verse. Have them guess the key word at the end of the drill. Here is a procedure to follow in conducting a Bible drill:

(The leader says the words in capitals.)
ATTENTION! (All participants get quiet and ready.)
BIBLES UP! (Participants grasp their Bibles by the bound edge and hold them up in the air.)
PROVERBS 21:24 (or whatever the reference is) Given twice.

Proverbs 21:24 (Participants repeat once.)
CHARGE! (Participants search for the verse in their Bibles. The first one who finds it stands. Leader waits until others are listening and has the winner read the verse.)

Five monster puppets are needed for these lessons. Each one characterizes a problem. These puppets may be made from the pattern and instructions given in Chapter Four for the shaggy dog or monster puppet. Add the features shown in Figure 45 to give the appropriate personality to your puppets.

Anger should be a red monster puppet. Envy or jealousy can be green. For the red and green monsters, add black shag for eyebrows, slanted as shown. Cut eyebrows according to pattern given in Figure 46. Use 30mm wiggle eyes on all monsters.

Fear or cowardice would be a yellow puppet. Worry and unhappiness is blue. For these two monsters, add large wiggle eyes and felt eyebrows as pictured—to give a scared or worried look.

Pride or selfishness is a purple monster with wiggle eyes and yellow felt eyelashes around eyes as pictured.

RED OR GREEN
MONSTER

YELLOW OR BLUE
MONSTER

PURPLE
MONSTER

Figure 45
The right eyebrows give monsters
appropriate expressions.

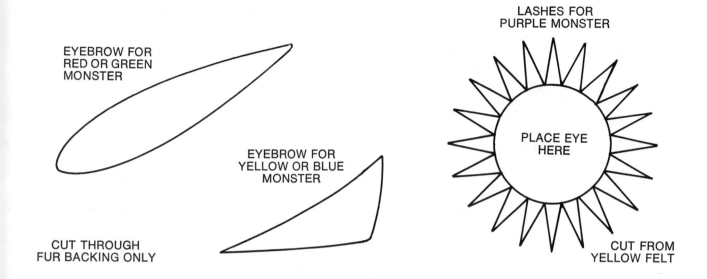

EYEBROW FOR
RED OR GREEN
MONSTER

CUT THROUGH
FUR BACKING ONLY

EYEBROW FOR
YELLOW OR BLUE
MONSTER

LASHES FOR
PURPLE MONSTER

PLACE EYE
HERE

CUT FROM
YELLOW FELT

Figure 46
Patterns for monster eyebrows and eyelashes.

Lesson 1—Anger

Bible Drill verses: Prov. 15:1; Col. 3:8; Eph. 4:26; Ps. 37:8

Puppet skit:

MONSTER   (Sticks head up, and looks around as if angry): What's going on here?

TEACHER: We're having _____ (Sunday School, etc.)

MONSTER: Well, I don't like it!

TEACHER: Why not?

MONSTER: Because everything makes me MAD!

TEACHER: Calm down.

MONSTER: Don't tell me what to do or I'll really get mean!

TEACHER: Who are you anyhow?

MONSTER: I'm the MAD MONSTER!

TEACHER: Do you have another name?

MONSTER: Some people call me Anger. Others call me Temper or Hate.

TEACHER: What do you do?

MONSTER: I make people say mean things and do mean things.

TEACHER: Why do you do that?

MONSTER: Because I'm a SIN!

TEACHER: Well, I don't want you to do that to me! Go away!

MONSTER: I'll go away now, but you wait. I'll be back to make you MAD!

POSSIBLE APPLICATION: What is anger or hatred anyhow? We could say that it is a strong feeling of revenge or wanting to get back at someone because of what he or she has done to us. It may be something they really did or something we just think they did.

Can you think of some people in the Bible who were angry with each other or hated someone? (Allow students to give examples.)

Use examples from one or more of these Bible stories: Cain and Abel (Gen. 4:2-15); Jacob and Esau (Gen. 27); Saul and David (1 Sam. 20). Point out why one man became angry with the other and how each reacted to the incident.

Boys and girls can have wrong kinds of anger toward other boys and girls, sisters and brothers, parents, and teachers. (Discuss situations for each of these.)

It is also a sin to make others angry. Sometimes we think it is fun to make someone mad by teasing or irritating him or her. God says this is wrong. When we really want to please God, we will not try to make others angry and we will not become angry with others. 1 Corinthians 13:5 says that if we love others we will be patient and not quick to be angry with them.

Is it ever right for us to be angry? Yes, we should be angry with sin and wrong in ourselves and others, but not angry with the person himself. (God loves the sinner, even though He hates the sinful behavior.)

How do we handle the wrong kind of anger?

First, realize it is sin. Second, remember that all sin needs to be forgiven. If you have never asked Jesus to be your Saviour, you need to believe that He died for your sin. Tell Him that you know you are a sinner and ask Him to forgive you and give you His gift of everlasting life. (See John 3:16.)

If you are already a Christian and have the sin of bad temper, hatred, or wrong anger in your heart, confess it (see 1 John 1:9) and ask God to keep you from it. Remember it is not up to you to get even for the wrong things others do to you (Rom. 12:19). Stay right with the Lord; He will help you do what is right.

Lesson 2—Fear

Bible Drill Verses: Ex. 14:13; Isa. 35:4; Heb. 13:6; Ps. 34:4

Puppet skit:

TEACHER: You can come out now.

MONSTER: No-o-o-o-o-o!

TEACHER: Why not?

MONSTER: I'm scared.

TEACHER: There's no reason to fear.

MONSTER: What do you mean? I am FEAR.

TEACHER: What do you do?

MONSTER: I make people fearful.

TEACHER: What do you want them to be afraid of?

MONSTER: Everything!

TEACHER: Why?

MONSTER: Because I am.

TEACHER: Are you really?

MONSTER: Y-Y-Yes . . .

TEACHER: Boo!

MONSTER: A-h-h-h-h-h-h!

TEACHER: Stay away. Your kind of fear is a sin.

POSSIBLE APPLICATION: Can you think of some other words for the wrong kind of fear? (dread, fright, scared, afraid, panic, terrified) We looked at some Bible verses that talk about the wrong kinds of fear. Let's look at some people in the Bible who had this kind of fear.

Our Bible examples show us at least four reasons for being fearful. (Discuss all briefly or just one at length.)

1. **Fear of God because of our sin.** Adam and Eve were the first to experience this kind of fear. (See Gen. 3:10.) God's remedy is found in 1 John 1:9. Ask Him to forgive you and cleanse you from sin. Then you needn't fear any longer because of the wrong you have done.

2. **Fear of things that might happen to us.** The Israelites were afraid they would not be able to conquer the land that God said would be theirs. (See Num. 13.) Because of their fear of man and unwillingness to believe and obey God, the Israelites had to wander in the desert for 40 years. God wants us to trust Him and do what He says. He has a plan for our lives (Rom. 8:28).

3. **Fear of what others will think of us.** We should be more concerned about what God thinks of us (Prov. 29:25). Peter denied Jesus because he was afraid of what others would think of him (Luke 22:54-62). How sorry he was when he realized what he had done.

4. **Fear of making a mistake or failing.** The Apostle Paul encouraged young Timothy. He told Timothy he should not be afraid (2 Tim. 1:7). If we are doing God's will, we need not be afraid of failing either. We must trust God to help us do things for His glory.

There is a right kind of fear—the fear of God. (Ps. 111:10; Prov. 10:27). If we have the right kind of fear, God can help us overcome the wrong kind. We must recognize that the wrong kind of fear is sin. Sin needs to be forgiven. Confess it, believe on the Lord Jesus Christ, and ask Him to forgive it and free him or her from fear (1 John 1:9).

Lesson 3—Envy or Jealousy

Bible Drill Verses—Prov. 14:30; Mark 15:10; Rom. 13:13; 1 Cor. 13:4; Rom. 1:29.

Puppet skit:

TEACHER: (Puppet shows himself) Who are you?

MONSTER: The Green Monster.

TEACHER: Do you have another name?

MONSTER: Jealousy! Envy!

TEACHER: What do you do to people?

MONSTER: I make them get angry at each other and hate one another.

TEACHER: Why do you do that?

MONSTER: Because I'm a sin.

TEACHER: I would like you to go away and not make any trouble.

POSSIBLE APPLICATION: How do you feel when someone can do something better than you can? (Most children will answer this question the way they think they should, not necessarily the way they really feel.)

Bill and Jack had always been good friends, but now in fifth grade something was going wrong with their friendship. You see, Bill tried out for the basketball team and made it. In fact, he was one of the best players. Jack had tried out for the team too, but somehow he just wasn't good enough. He practiced at home for a while, but finally he gave up.

He and Bill didn't see as much of each other as before. Jack went back to doing what he and Bill had done before basketball season. That was building model cars and planes. Jack was really good at putting things together. He would spend hours making plans and then the models.

Jack began to notice, though, that Bill was very popular at school. He wished he was getting the attention Bill was getting. Jack's mother noticed the change in Jack and asked him what was wrong.

"I wish I was good in sports like Bill. I can't do anything right," he complained.

Mom reminded him how good he was at making models. But somehow what she said didn't seem to help Jack. None of the kids at school knew how good he was at building model planes and cars. All they cared about was how good a guy was at sports.

Bill began to notice a change in Jack too. Jack hardly spoke anymore. On Saturday when Bill came over, Jack was unfriendly. Jack began to say things in front of others that really hurt Bill's feelings.

What do you think was wrong with Jack? (Allow time for discussion. Make sure the children conclude that Jack was jealous of Bill.) What should you do when you feel envious of someone?

Remember that envy or jealously is sin. Sin needs to be forgiven. The unsaved person needs to accept Christ. The Christian must confess and be cleansed of his sin (1 John 1:9).

How can you keep from being jealous?

Remember that God made you like you are. He wants to use what you can do. You are special. Never mind what someone else is able to do. Follow Jesus and be grateful for the talents He has given you. Be glad for the abilities or things He has given others.

What should you do when someone is jealous of you? Pray that God will help him get over it. Be friendly and point out to him that God has given him special abilities too. If he is not a Christian, try to win him to Jesus.

Lesson 4—Worry or Unhappiness

Bible Drill Verses—Job 34:29; Ps. 77:2, 4; Ps. 46:1; Ps. 34:6, 17; John 14:1a

Puppet Skit:

TEACHER (Puppet begins to appear as you speak): What's your name?

MONSTER: Sob, sob, sob, sob!

TEACHER: Do you have a name?

(Monster sobs violently.)

TEACHER: Who are you?

MONSTER: I'm worry, unhappiness, trouble, sorrow, sadness, misery, self-pity. O-h-h-h-h!

TEACHER: Hold it! Are you all those things?

MONSTER: Y-y-y-y-y-es, I'm the b-b-b-blues and o-o-oh!

TEACHER: What do you do to people?

MONSTER: I make them unhappy and miserable, just like me.

TEACHER: Why, how do you do that?

MONSTER: I get them to worry and feel sorry for themselves and get in trouble, and . . .

TEACHER: Stop! That's enough. I get the idea. We don't need you here. Go away.

MONSTER: I-I-I will. Bad night (or day).

POSSIBLE APPLICATION: Do you ever feel sorry for yourself? Do you ever worry about something bad happening to you? If we let feelings of worry and unhappiness stay in our minds, they can make us miserable. Sometimes trouble makes us unhappy.

The Book of Job tells us about a man who had lots of trouble. (Study the facts of Job's life and tell some of the trials and troubles he had.) So many bad things happened to Job that his wife told him to curse God and die. Job had a good reason for being sad and sorrowful, but he still trusted God. Later on God blessed Job with more happiness and wealth than before his trouble.

Every person has trouble of one kind or another. Sometimes a friend or loved one dies and we are sorry or sad. That's not a wrong kind of sadness, but even then we need to trust God and ask Him to help us.

Sometimes God lets accidents, disappointments, or things which seem unjust happen to us so that we will learn to trust Him more. He wants us to "cast our care on Him."

God doesn't want us to be unhappy and worry over what might happen to us. He wants each of us to know Him as our own Saviour. Then He promises to be with us always.

Sometimes we worry and are unhappy because of our sin. When we do wrong things, it always gets us into trouble. That's when we need to ask God to forgive us. When we are right with the Lord, He gives us peace and joy in place of worry and unhappiness.

Lesson 5—Pride and Selfishness

Bible Drill Verses: Ps. 10:4; Prov. 13:10; 8:13; 6:16-17; 21:4; 16:18; 1 Peter 5:5; Mark 7:20-23

Puppet skit:

MONSTER (Singing): La-de-da-de-da! I'm so beautiful and I'm so good! Well, well what have we here?

TEACHER: We're having _____ (Sunday School, etc.).

MONSTER: And what, pray tell, is _____?

TEACHER: We study the Bible.

MONSTER: Well, I don't need that. I'm good enough.

TEACHER: No one is good enough.

MONSTER: Well, I am. I'm the most beautiful, smartest, strongest, I am the BEST!

TEACHER: You are a sin!

MONSTER: That's true, but I don't like to admit it, and I want everyone to think just as I do.

TEACHER: What do you do?

MONSTER: I kill people with selfishness and pride.

POSSIBLE APPLICATION: Pride is thinking you are better than others in some area of your life: looks, abilities, advantages.

The Bible gives many examples of people who were proud. Cain, King Saul Saul of Tarsus are a few. King Saul was good-looking and was given power to rule his people. He became proud. Cain was proud because he was a good farmer. He thought he was good enough and didn't need to obey God.

Saul of Tarsus was proud. He thought he knew what God wanted and that God wanted him to persecute Christians. (These examples could be developed in some depth for this lesson, showing the results of pride and how God dealt with it. The parable of the Pharisee and the Publican could also be used.)

What can you do about pride and selfishness? Realize pride is sin. Say "I'm sorry" to God and believe that He will forgive you for Jesus' sake. Ask the Lord to help you overcome it (James 4:6). Remember we are all sinners in His sight (Isa. 64:6). Live in an attitude of humility toward others (they are better—Phil. 2:3; love them—Matt. 19:19). Any special "talents," looks, or things you have are from God and He wants you to use them for His sake.

What do you do about others who act proud?

Be kind to them. Pray that they will receive Jesus as their Saviour. If they are Christians, pray that they will allow the Lord to lead or direct them.

JIM'S VICTORY

Theme: Fear of failing (Juniors and young teens)
Characters: Jim, Yellow Monster, and Greg
Settings: Outdoors

Figure 47
The monster FEAR whispers to Jim in "Jim's Victory."

(Greg and Jim appear from one side. They're panting and moving slowly as if out of breath.)

GREG   (Stops and looks at Jim): Wow! That was a good race!

JIM   (Nods): You're not kidding! I'm out of breath.

GREG   (Tips head): Jim, you're good at a lot of things. You always try so hard. How come?

YELLOW MONSTER   (Appears behind Jim): Don't tell him. He'll think you're an oddball.

JIM: Well, er, ah, well it's because . . .

GREG   (Looks away from Jim): Oh, never mind. I didn't mean to put you on the spot. Hey, I'll see you later. I've got a lot of homework. (Greg leaves.)

JIM   (Shakes his head sadly): I'm such a failure. I had the perfect chance to tell Greg about the Lord and I blew it!

YELLOW MONSTER   (Leans over him): That's all right. If you tell him about being a Christian he won't be your friend anymore.

JIM   (His head down): Let's see. What are some of those verses I learned that would help me speak up for the Lord?

YELLOW MONSTER   (Shakes head): Forget it, Jim. With me around, those verses won't help you.

JIM   (Moving his head back and forth as if thinking hard): I've just got to get over being afraid to speak about the Lord. I'll remember those verses and pray that I won't be afraid. (Looks around as if trying to remember) Yeah, that's one. "Be strong and courageous; do not tremble or be dismayed, for the Lord your God is with you wherever you go" (Josh. 1:9, NASB). Lord, please help me tell Greg about You.

MONSTER   (Throws his head back in frustration and leaves as he speaks): Oh, no! I'm a goner!

GREG   (Comes back as Jim looks up): Hi, Jim. I forgot my books. I wouldn't have gotten much homework done without them.

JIM   (Moves over to Greg): Hey, Greg, you know that question you asked me before—about why I try so hard? I'd sure like to talk to you about that. Mind if I walk along with you?

GREG   (Shakes head): Not at all. I'd be glad if you did. I have some other questions I'd like to ask too.

POSSIBLE APPLICATION: What do you think those other questions might be? I think maybe Greg is ready to hear about the Lord, don't you?

We Christians need to ask the Lord to help us speak up for Him and not be afraid to tell our unsaved friends about Him.

WORRISOME WENDY

Theme: Worry
Characters: Wendy, Blue Monster, Sharon
Setting: School playground. School has just let out for the day.

BLUE MONSTER   (Appears as Wendy comes into view): Oh good! Here she comes now.

WENDY   (Stands with head bent. Shakes as if sobbing): Oh, boohoo, boohoo! (Looks up as she speaks sadly): I'm so miserable. I just know I got a bad grade in that spelling test. Everyone's going to think I'm dumb!

BLUE MONSTER   (Speaks to Wendy sadly. She does not act as if she sees him): That's right, Wendy. There's no hope for you. You might as well give up.

(Wendy bends down and sobs some more.)

(Sharon appears and monster leaves.)

SHARON   (Tips head to look at Wendy): What's wrong, Wendy? Why are you crying?

WENDY   (Still sobbing): Oh, Sharon, I think I got a bad grade on the spelling test and that's not all . . .

BLUE MONSTER   (Appears behind girls. They don't see him. Speaks in a sad voice to Wendy): You tell her, Wendy. There's so much to worry about. Maybe Sharon will get discouraged too. (He leaves.)

WENDY: I heard on the news there might be a food shortage (or some crisis that will apply to your group). What if _____ happens to me?

SHARON: Wendy, you shouldn't worry about things like that.

BLUE MONSTER   (Appears near Wendy): Yes, you should, Wendy.

WENDY   (Looks at Sharon): Why shouldn't I worry?

SHARON   (Tips head as if thinking): Well, because God will be with us no matter what happens. You need to learn to trust Him.

WENDY   (Shakes head): But it's so hard. Tell me how to trust Him more, Sharon.

BLUE MONSTER   (Shakes head): No, don't listen to her, Wendy. Listen to me.

WENDY   (Moves closer to Sharon away from monster): How can I stop worrying?

SHARON: Wendy, you must trust God for everything. He loves you and wants you to "cast all your care upon Him for He cares for you."

BLUE MONSTER   (Goes away with his head down): Oh no; I think I'm going to lose another worrier.

WENDY   (Moves excitedly): Sharon, thanks! I had forgotten that Bible verse. I know I shouldn't worry. I'll trust the Lord about my spelling test. I did my best. (Wendy and Sharon leave.)

POSSIBLE APPLICATION: The Bible says in Romans 8:28 that "we know that all things work together for good to them that love God, to them who are the called according to His purpose." God cares for every Christian and has a purpose for everything that happens in a Christian's life. He wants us to trust Him completely. That's the way we can win over the monster called Worry.

MARK'S MADNESS

> Theme: Anger
> Characters: Mark, Johnny, Dad, Red Monster, Green Monster
> Setting: A living room

DAD   (Comes in and looks around): Now, where are those boys? Mark! Where are you?

MARK   (Comes in quickly): Oh, hi, Dad! What's the matter?

DAD: Mark, I just drove the car into the drive and almost ran over your bike. How many times have I told you boys to put your bikes away when you finish using them?

MARK   (Shakes his head): But, Dad, I did put it away. Why don't you ask Johnny about it? He takes my bike out and forgets to put it back.

DAD   (Tips head to one side): Are you saying that your little brother did it?

MARK   (Nods) Yeah, Dad, honest!

DAD   (Turns to leave): I'll speak to him about it!

MARK   (Paces back and forth): Yeah! He'll speak to him about it. That little brother of mine gets away with everything and I get blamed.

RED MONSTER   (Appears behind Mark. Speaks in an angry tone): I wouldn't put up with it! You've got your rights. Your Dad shouldn't push you around on account of that little brother of yours.

MARK: Dad'll probably just pat him on the head and say, "Daddy's little boy mustn't be naughty."

RED MONSTER   (Nods): That's right, Mark. Get mad at him.

(Green monster appears on Mark's other side.)

MARK: It just makes me so mad! Mom and Dad even got him a better bike than mine and he still insists on using mine and getting me in trouble by not putting it away.

GREEN MONSTER   (Speaks in Mark's ear): It's not fair. You should have had the better bike. After all, you're older.

MARK   (Moves back and forth): U-u-u-u-u-h-h-h-h-h! I'm so mad!
(Green and Red Monsters move about happily.)

RED MONSTER: I'm so glad you're angry at your brother.

GREEN MONSTER: And I'm so glad you're jealous of him! (Dad and Johnny come in. Monsters duck out of sight.)

DAD: Mark, I want to say I'm sorry for bawling you out. Johnny admitted he left your bike out and has something to say to you.

JOHNNY   (Looks up at Mark): Mark, I'm sorry for using your bike without asking you. I have an idea, though. You know my bike is newer than yours, and I know you like it a lot.

MARK: Yeah, I like your bike. What about it?

JOHNNY: Well, don't you see? I like your bike better too. Why don't we trade?
(Both boys look at Dad.)

DAD   (Nods): It's up to you two. I just don't want you to fight about it later. A deal is a deal.
(Boys look at each other.)

JOHNNY: OK?

MARK   (Hesitates for a moment and then nods): OK!

(Green and Red Monsters appear cautiously and speak to Mark.)

GREEN MONSTER: He'll probably back out on the deal.

RED MONSTER: Yeah, don't trust him!

MARK   (To Johnny): You know, Johnny, I had some pretty mean thoughts about you. I'm sorry.

MONSTERS   (Fall back and disappear): Oh, no!

JOHNNY   (Lowers head): And I'm sorry for making you angry.

DAD   (Stands up straight): That's music to my ears!

MARK   (Starts to leave): Come on, Johnny, let's go try out our "new" bikes.

POSSIBLE APPLICATION: Things turned out all right for these brothers. Anger and Jealousy were defeated. The Bible tells us about some brothers who let anger and jealousy win in their lives. Joseph's brothers were jealous of him and became so angry that they sold him as a slave. If it had not been for God's care and goodness, Joseph could have died. (Study the story of Joseph in Gen. 37, 39–47.)

DEBBY'S PURPLE PRIDE

Theme: Pride
Characters: Debby, Debby's mother, Joan, Purple Monster, a boy, a girl, Miss Jenkins, other boy and girl puppets if desired.

Setting: Scene One—A living room
Scenes Two and Three—A school classroom

(The puppet characters in this skit do not notice the purple monster. He is symbolic of Debby's pride. As the first scene opens, Debby is facing the wall on one side of the room. Her head is down. She is writing.)

MOTHER   (Her voice is heard but she is not seen): Debby, did you finish writing your poem for the contest?

DEBBY   (Answers without looking up): Yes, Mother, I don't know what the big deal is. I always win the contest anyhow.

PURPLE MONSTER   (Appears on stage and stands behind Debby): That's right, Debby. You are THE BEST! No doubt about it. You don't even have to work hard to be a winner.

DEBBY   (Doesn't see monster): Boy, this is a snap! Miss Jenkins knows I'm the best poem writer in the class. How can anyone else have a chance?

PURPLE MONSTER (Nods): You tell 'em, Sweetie! You're better than everyone.

DEBBY   (Moves to center stage and moves her head around as she talks): Well that's it! It might not be the best poem I ever wrote, but it'll sure be better than the others.

(Purple monster nods his head and leaves.)

MOTHER   (Comes in): Oh, did you finish your poem, dear? May I read it?

DEBBY   (Starts to leave): Not now, Mother. I have to get to school early. Bye.

MOTHER   (Tilts head to one side and watches Debby leave): Good-bye, dear.

SCENE 2   (Empty school classroom)

DEBBY   (Comes in looking all around): Good! I'm the first one here.

PURPLE MONSTER   (Comes in and stands behind Debby, as she finishes speaking. He speaks proudly and leaves as Joan comes in): You always are first, aren't you? You're first at everything. You're the best student in the class, the best . . .

JOAN   (Comes in quickly, speaks excitedly): Oh, hi, Debby. I'm so glad you're here. I worked hard on my poem. I know it won't be as good as yours, but I'd be happy even if it won second or third prize.

DEBBY   (Tips head to one side and "talks down" to Joan): Oh really? That good. huh? How nice. Too bad I won't have time to read it and give you some hints. Here comes Miss Jenkins.

MISS JENKINS   (Speaks as she enters): Good morning, girls. My, you're here early. Are your poems ready?

JOAN and DEBBY   (Nod their heads and speak together): Yes!

MISS JENKINS   (Nods her head and moves toward girls): Good! If you will let me have them, I'll take them to the office right now.

(Joan and Debby move about as if to get their papers out. Then they move toward Miss Jenkins.)

DEBBY   (Tips her head to one side and speaks proudly): Here it is, Miss Jenkins.

JOAN   (Speaks quietly as she moves hesitantly toward Miss Jenkins): Here's mine too, Miss Jenkins.

MISS JENKINS   (Turns to leave): I'll get these right to the office.

SCENE 3   (Several days later at school. Some boy and girl puppets, including Debby and Joan, are facing Miss Jenkins.)

MISS JENKINS   (Moves around as if excited): Good morning, class. I have some exciting and surprising news for you.

DEBBY   (Looks toward audience and nods head as the purple monster appears behind her. He appears to be laughing, though no sound is heard. After Debby speaks, both she and the monster turn and face Miss Jenkins): Here it comes! Another victory for ME!

MISS JENKINS   (Tilts head): Our class should feel very honored. Not only did one of our members win the school poetry contest. This person also won the contest for the whole district!

(Purple Monster stretches up taller.)

DEBBY   (Also stretches up taller): Here it comes.

MISS JENKINS: The winner is—JOAN. Congratulations, Joan. I have a special ribbon and a certificate for you.

(Joan moves toward Miss Jenkins timidly as the others clap.)

(Debby opens mouth and stares straight ahead.)

PURPLE MONSTER   (Falls on side as if wounded): A-a-a-a-a-a-h-h-h!

GIRL   (Looking at Debby and moving up and down): Miss Jenkins, Miss Jenkins, what's wrong with Debby? She's staring straight ahead with her mouth open.

BOY   (Hopping up and down): I think I know. Her PRIDE just died! Hey, I'm a poet too!

BIBLE CHARACTERS WHO WERE PROUD: Haman (Esther); King Saul (1 Sam.); a Pharisee (Luke 18:10-14)

Figure 48
A scene from "Debby's Purple Pride"

POSSIBLE APPLICATION: Did you know that the Bible says that pride goes before a fall? (Prov. 16:18) Debby had a monster in her life called PRIDE that made her fall. A lot of people are proud, and being proud does not please God. 1 Peter 5:5 says that God resists or is against the proud person. Pride often keeps people from asking the Lord to be their Saviour. They don't think they're bad enough to need a Saviour, but the Bible says "For all have sinned and come short of the glory of God" (Rom. 3:23).

Pride can even be a problem for Christians. It keeps them from loving and obeying God and loving others as they should.

God can help each of us win a victory over pride. The first step toward that victory is receiving Jesus as your Saviour—admitting you are a sinner and need His forgiveness. If you have accepted Jesus, but have let pride take over, ask Him to forgive you.

A BASEBALL MITT FOR BOBBY

Theme: Trusting, stealing, being tempted

Characters: Bobby, Mother, Mr. Hanson

Setting: Scene One—A living room
Scene Two—A sporting goods store (baseball mitts visible)
Scene Three—A living room

BOBBY   (Comes into the room as he speaks): Hi Mom! I'm home and guess what?

MOTHER   (Enters): What?

BOBBY: Our class is starting a baseball team and I tried out today and I made it!

MOTHER: That's wonderful, Bobby. I'm so proud of you.

BOBBY: Only one thing though, Mom.

MOTHER: What's that?

BOBBY: Well, we're going to play our first game tomorrow and you have to sign a permission slip.

MOTHER: Oh, I'll be happy to do that.

BOBBY   (Hesitates): Well er-ah that's not all, Mom. I have to have a baseball mitt or I can't play. I have some money of my own but I think I'll need a little more to get the mitt.

MOTHER: Oh dear, Bobby, how much do you need?

BOBBY: About $4.

MOTHER: Bobby, I'd just love to give you $4, but your father doesn't get paid until Friday. We've had a lot of extra bills this month. I'm sorry, Bobby, I just don't have $4 to give you.

BOBBY: Oh, no! That means I can't be on the team.

MOTHER: Bobby, you know the Lord understands your problem. Why don't you talk to Him? (Mother leaves.)

BOBBY: Oh, what am I going to do? The Lord's not interested in a boy's baseball mitt. He's got bigger things on His mind. (Bobby walks away with his head down as the scene ends.)

SCENE 2   (Setting: Mr. Hanson's sporting goods store)

MR. HANSON: (Comes in from left as Bobby comes in from right.) Well, young man, what can I do for you?

BOBBY: I'd like to look at the baseball mitts.

MR. HANSON: They're right over there, Bobby. I'll be with you in a minute. I have a customer in the fishing gear department. (Mr. Hanson leaves.)

BOBBY   (Stares at the mitts): Boy, Mr. Hanson sure has a lot of baseball mitts. I'll bet he wouldn't even miss one. (Moves closer to the mitts.) It wouldn't really be stealing because when I got the money, I'd come back and pay him for it. (Moves closer to mitts.) But I might get caught. Then I'd be in trouble. (Looks in the direction Mr. Hanson left.) Mr. Hanson wouldn't need to know. I could stick it under my jacket. (Moves closer again.) NO! I can't do that. The Bible says not to steal. I never stole anything, and I'm not going to now. Maybe if I talk to Mr. Hanson, he'll let me have the glove and pay the $4 later.

MR. HANSON   (Comes in and stands by Bobby): Well, young fella, which one did you decide to take?

BOBBY: Er-ah-ah-ah—I decided not to take any. I was wondering if we could make a deal, Mr. Hanson.

MR. HANSON: What kind of a deal, Bobby?

BOBBY: Well, I need a baseball mitt by tomorrow or I can't be on the team. I've got almost enough money for it. Mr. Hanson, do you think you could let me have the mitt now for the money I have and I'll pay you the rest later?

MR. HANSON   (Shakes his head): Well now, Bobby, this presents a problem. If I do that for you, every boy in town will be in here trying to make a deal.

BOBBY: But Mr. Hanson, you go to our church and all, and I thought maybe . . .

MR. HANSON: I know, Bobby. I think the world of you and your family. Tell me, have you asked the Lord to help you solve your problem?

BOBBY   (Shakes his head): No, I just can't see how He cares about a baseball mitt.

MR. HANSON: God cares about everything in our lives.

BOBBY: But, Mr. Hanson, I thought of stealing one of these mitts. God doesn't help people who steal.

MR. HANSON: Bobby, I know you're a Christian. I think the Lord kept you from stealing. I'm pretty sure too, that if He wants you to have a mitt you'll have it.

BOBBY: Thanks for not being mad at me. I'll try to trust the Lord more. (He leaves.)

MR. HANSON   (Turns to corner as if using the telephone): Hello Ruth. (pause) You remember those things our boy John outgrew? (pause) Yeah, that big box. Wasn't there a baseball mitt in there? (pause) Oh good! Are you real busy? (pause) Good! I have a little errand for you to do right away. (Continues speaking as scene ends.)

SCENE 3   (Bobby's Living Room)

BOBBY   (Comes in with his head down.): OK, Lord. I'm going to trust You. If You want me to be on the baseball team, I know You'll make a way for me to get a mitt. If You don't want me on the team, help me to be happy anyhow. Amen. (Looks up.) There! That's settled. Am I glad I didn't steal that mitt. I would have felt awful. (Looks around.) Mo-o-om!

MOTHER   (Comes in excitedly): Oh, Bobby, I'm glad you're home. I have a wonderful surprise for you.

BOBBY: What is it?

MOTHER: Just a little while ago Mrs. Hanson was here and she brought something for you. (Bobby and mother move slightly to the corner and look down. Bobby moves as if excited.)

BOBBY: Wow! Look at all that neat stuff! And a baseball mitt right on the top. It's almost like the one I wanted to buy. I'm going to phone the Hansons right away and thank them. You know, Mom, God answered my prayer—through them.

MARTHA'S MONEY

> Theme: Lying
>
> Characters: Martha, Cindy, Mother

Setting: Scene One—living room
　　　　 Scene Two—outdoors
　　　　 Scene Three—living room

MOTHER   (Looking out the window as Martha comes into room): Hi, honey, are you all ready for school?

MARTHA: Yes! I'm walking with Cindy. Mom, can I have 50c for school?

MOTHER: I just gave you money for school yesterday and the day before. What's the money for today?

MARTHA: Well, er-ah we're collecting money for poor people.

MOTHER: Oh, how nice. Are you sure 50c is enough?

MARTHA: Well, we can give more if we want.

MOTHER   (Goes out as if to get some money. Comes back and hands it to Martha): Here you are, dear. Have a nice day at school.

MARTHA: Bye, Mom.

SCENE 2   (Outdoors, Martha and Cindy are walking together.)

CINDY: Did you get some money for after school?

MARTHA: Yep! Nothin' to it. I just told Mom we were collecting for poor people.

CINDY: You mean you lied to your mom?

MARTHA: Sure. She never knows the difference. After school we'll stop by the ice-cream store to get a treat.

CINDY: No thanks, Martha. I don't think I want a treat from money you got by lying.

MARTHA: Well, of all the stupid things. How do you think I got the money for the other treats?

CINDY: You mean you lied to get that money too?

MARTHA: Oh be quiet! I'll find someone else to go with me to the ice-cream store.

CINDY: Wait, Martha, I didn't mean to make you mad. I'll go with you, but why don't I buy the treats for a while. My mother gives me money for chores sometimes.

MARTHA: It's up to you.

SCENE 3 (Living room)

MOTHER (Stands off to one side and appears to be talking on the telephone): Yes, Miss Thomas, I'll be glad to have a conference with you about Martha. By the way, it's so nice that you're collecting money for the needy. (pause) You're not? But Martha told me . . . Oh, that's why you wanted to talk to me. Does she do this often? (pause) Yes, I'm beginning to see that she has a problem. I certainly will speak to her about it. Thank you for calling. I'll see you Friday afternoon.

MARTHA (Comes in as Mother turns to look at her): Hi, Mom. You know what?

MOTHER: What?

MARTHA: We're going on a field trip Friday, and I need to have my dollar in tomorrow.

MOTHER: I'm sorry, Martha. I'm afraid I can't give you a dollar.

MARTHA: But why? You always give me money.

MOTHER: Yes, I have been giving you money, but no more. Martha, why did you tell me all those stories about needing money?

MARTHA: I-I-I . . .

MOTHER: How do I know you're telling the truth now? Maybe there isn't any field trip.

MARTHA (Pleadingly): Yes there is a field trip, Mom. There really is. If I don't bring my money, I'll have to sit in the principal's office. I'm sorry I lied the other times.

MOTHER: Martha, it's time you learned that lying hurts yourself and others. We'll talk about the field trip later.

DOUG DISOBEYS

> Theme: Disobedience
> Characters: Doug, Mother, Father, Buster—the Dog
> Setting: Living room (As scene opens Doug is looking down as if coloring.)

DOUG: Boy, am I hungry. I wonder when we're gonna eat?

MOTHER (Her voice is heard, but she is not seen.): Doug, it's time to get ready for dinner. Your dad will be here soon. Be sure and put those crayons away before we eat.

DOUG (Continues what he has been doing): OK, Mom.

MOTHER (Comes in): Doug, please get ready for dinner. Did you remember to put your roller skates away this afternoon?

DOUG: Don't worry about it, Mom. I'll do it.
(A crash is heard, followed by some bumps.)

FATHER (His voice is heard but he is not seen): O-h-h-h-h! (Loudly) Doug! Come here this minute!

DOUG: Uh, oh! I think Dad found my skates. (Turns to leave.)

FATHER (Comes in before Doug gets out of the room): Doug, where are your skates supposed to be kept when you aren't using them?

DOUG: On the shelf in the garage.

FATHER: Then why were they on the front sidewalk?

DOUG: 'Cause I guess I left them there.

FATHER: Right! When are you going to learn to obey and take care of your things?

MOTHER (Comes in toward Father): Are you hurt, dear?

FATHER: No, I'll be all right.

MOTHER: Doug, it's time to eat. Please put your crayons away now and meet us at the table. (Mother and Father leave.)

DOUG: OK. (Doug leaves in the opposite direction from his parents without doing anything about the crayons. His dog Buster comes in. He tosses the crayons into the air and makes little barking sounds as the scene ends.)

SCENE 2   Same as the end of First scene. (Buster is still playing with the crayons.)

FATHER (His voice is heard but he is not seen): Boy, that was a good dinner. Right, Doug?

DOUG (From off stage): It sure was! (Comes in but stops suddenly when he sees Buster with the crayons.) You dumb dog! Get away from those crayons. (Buster runs out of the room.) Oh, what a mess! All my crayons are broken.

FATHER (Comes in): What did you say was broken?

DOUG: My crayons. (Moves up and down as if picking them up.) That dumb dog.

FATHER: Now wait a minute, Doug. I heard your mother tell you to put the crayons away before dinner. You know Buster is still a pup and chews things.

DOUG: I know—I'm going out to ride my bike for a little while.

MOTHER (Comes in): All right, but be sure to put it away when you finish riding it.

DOUG: OK. (Turns to leave.)

FATHER (Turns to Mother as he speaks): I see our son is having trouble taking responsibility. We're going to have to see to it that he learns to obey.

MOTHER (Nods agreement): You're right, dear. I just hope he doesn't have to learn the hard way.

FATHER: Well, I better get ready for my meeting with Mr. Scott. (Father turns to leave as Mother looks out the window. Then she turns to leave too.)

FATHER (Comes in; calls to Mother): I'm leaving now. I should be home around 9 o'clock.

MOTHER (Comes in): All right, dear. See you later.
(Another crash is heard and Father reappears after a little while. As he enters Mother rushes to meet him.)

FATHER (Impatiently): Well, that did it! Doug has no more bike. He left it right in the middle of the driveway behind the car. Doug, come here.

DOUG (Comes in): What's wrong, Dad?

FATHER: Doug, you don't have a bike anymore.

DOUG (Moves back in surprise): But—what happened? Uh-oh! I didn't put it away, did I?

FATHER: That's right. And it's a pretty expensive way to learn why you should obey, isn't it?

(Doug nods his head in agreement, sadly.)

OTHER RESOURCE MATERIAL

Chapter One
—STROM, ROBERT D. *Growing Together*. Monterey, Calif.: Books/Cole, 1978
—ZUCK, ROY B. and CLARK, ROBERT E. (eds.) *Childhood Education in the Church*. Chicago: Moody Press, 1975.

Chapter Three
—RICHARDS, LARRY O. *Creative Bible Teaching*. Chicago: Moody Press, 1970.

Chapter Four
—GREEN, LEE. *Teaching Tools You Can Make*. Wheaton, Ill.: Victor Books, 1978

Chapter Seven
—HANFORD, ROBERT TEN EYCK, *The Complete Book of Puppets and Puppeteering*. New York and London: Drake Publishers, 1976.

Chapter Nine
—MARTIN, SHIRLEY; MARTIN, CYNTHIA S. *Who Ever Saw a Pink Hippo?* Wheaton, Ill.: Scripture Press Publications, 1978.
—MARTIN, CYNTHIA S.; FOX, GRACE, *Sorry, Suzy, Not Today*. Wheaton, Ill.: Scripture Press Publications, 1978.
—HORTON, JANET; FOX, GRACE, *King of the Beasts*. Wheaton, Ill.: Scripture Press Publications, 1978.

Delightful, loveable SPuppets make it easier for you to pass on God's truths to people—little and large. The full body puppets—Peggy Panda, Reginald Rabbit, Susy Squirrel, and Lester Lamb—enable you to bring them to life on your hand or sit them down like a toy. Their heads and front legs move. The large, sleeve puppets—Larney Lion and Hoby Hippo—move mouths and roll eyes. All SPuppets are made of cuddly, furry cloth that is cleanable and dryable.

SUBJECT INDEX FOR SCRIPTS